G/ATA
ROME

NAPLES

THE TESIOS, as I knew them

THE TESIOS

as I knew them

by

Mario Incisa

J. A. ALLEN & CO. LTD.

London and New York

First published in 1979
by J. A. Allen & Co.
1 Lower Grosvenor Place
London SW1W 0EL

© 1979 Mario Incisa

British Library Cataloguing in Publication Data
Incisa, Mario
    The Tesios as I knew them.
    1. Tesio, Federico   2. Horse breeders – Italy
    – Biography
    I. Title
    636.1'2'0924   SF336.T/
    ISBN 0–85131–313–2

Set printed and bound in Great Britain
by Billing and Sons Limited
Guildford, London, Oxford, Worcester

Contents

CHAPTER 1

I meet the Tesios

IT WAS TESIO himself whom I met first—not at the races nor even in connection with horses—but casually, at the Hotel Plaza in Rome.

It must have been 1923 or 1924, during my student days. Giorgio Ugolino della Gherardesca, who was studying with me at Pisa University and whose cousin I was later to marry, had come to visit me in Rome. We were strolling down the Corso, just approaching the Plaza, when Giorgio Ugolino suddenly said: 'Come, I will introduce you to Tesio—but for heaven's sake don't mention horses!' As we entered the hotel the hall porter informed us that Tesio was in the hall. The Gherardescas were old friends of the Tesios so we approached without waiting to be announced.

Tesio was sunk deep in an armchair reading a book; it may have been his split-pedigree book or it may have been one of the detective stories which he devoured by the dozen. On seeing us he exclaimed: 'Hello ... how are you?' in a curious falsetto. Being so often lost in his own thoughts, his face usually carried a rather forbidding frown but he knew the ways of the world sufficiently to show a certain smiling surprise at a casual meeting and emphasised this, intentionally or otherwise, by the falsetto.

Tesio remained seated in his armchair whilst giving each of us a handshake which was strangely limp for a man well-known for his energy and vitality. His eyes, which had seemed lifeless while he was reading, lit up in cheerful anticipation and a rapid exchange of conventional questions and answers about the entire Gherardesca family occurred before I was finally introduced. During that brief conversation I noticed that Tesio still had a slight Piedmontese accent and used expressions which were typical of his native region. On hearing my name he commented: 'Piedmontese, eh?' His remark rather flattered me (it always gives pleasure that one's name should mean something to one's questioner), but I felt that it also revealed that his accent and use of local words were due, not only to his origins, but also to a certain pride in having been born and brought up in Piemonte.

So *this* was Tesio, to whom on no account was any mention of horses to be made. Had I not known who he was, the last subject it would have occurred to me to discuss with him would have been horses! I had a clear image of how a horseman should look—unmistakable and stereotyped; Tesio was the antithesis of this. He seemed more like a notary, a doctor or an unfrocked priest: short, stocky, his head sunk into his slightly curved shoulders. Hardly the model of a master of foxhounds, a cavalry colonel or an adept of the Sport of Kings! And I should add (alas!) that Tesio's eyes, which were extraordinarily lively and intelligent, further accentuated his difference from the stereotype.

The conversation cannot have lasted for more than a quarter-of-an-hour and to say that I was greatly impressed by my first meeting with Tesio would be far from the truth. I had been far more excited before, when Giorgio Ugolino had said: 'Come, I will introduce you to Tesio.' Tesio was just a man like any other. To discover this after all I had heard said about him, with such admiration, was rather disappointing.

I did not meet Tesio again until 1929, though it would have been easy for me to do so. For several years I lived in the same hotel as the Tesios, the Nettuno, in Pisa. Not wishing to push myself forward on the strength of our brief acquaintance, I preferred to avoid them.

The occasion of our second meeting had as little to do with horses as our first. Mutual friends had decided to introduce me, through Donna Lydia, to the girl who was later to become my wife: half a century ago it was still customary to make use of such solicitous and, whatever may be said today, useful, matchmakers. So an absurdly contrived meeting between Clarice della Gherardesca and myself was to be the beginning of my association with the Tesios. That meeting put me firmly, not only under Donna Lydia's supervision, but also under her protection. It was the year of Cavaliere d'Arpino and I remember being fully aware of the honour bestowed upon me when I was admitted into the box of the champion on the eve of the Omnium, which was to be his last race. Tesio was examining Cavaliere d'Arpino's troublesome leg with some concern.

Tesio tolerated me in the stables although he did not at that time appear to notice my presence. It was Donna Lydia who, feeling responsible for having discovered and introduced me, took infinite pains to have me meet my future fiancée on every conceivable pretext: our mutual passion for horses provided the necessary excuse for our frequent encounters at the Tesios. Once again the Hotel Nettuno became home to me. No longer the little room on the fourth floor but the Tesio's private apartment, where we would lunch when there were races (Tesio himself was never there), and have tea after the races (Tesio would be there if he had had a winner), but I was not yet admitted to their country house and stud-farm at Dormello.

In May, 1930, to Donna Lydia's great relief (for she was an enthusiastic matchmaker), my official engagement to Clarice della Gherardesca was finally announced and the doors of Dormello were opened to me. It was arranged that I should go there for the first time during that summer. My fiancée and her father were to be there: all had been well planned in accordance with the conventions of the time and the traditions of 'society'.

Of that first visit I remember only the incredibly green paddocks, the house covered with a thick blanket of ivy and a slight but penetrating stable smell which pervaded the atmosphere outside and inside the house. Tesio vaguely emanated the same odour; it came from his shoes.

It was impossible to get a word in first about Dormello. Donna Lydia was so proud of the place and so much in love with it that she was the first to point out all its advantages and to sing its praises. For Tesio, on the other hand, it was a means to an end; it was instrumental in producing his horses. He was completely unsentimental about Dormello and, in fact, spent little time there.

I had imagined that it would be like the conventional studs of the time, built around a central yard, and was surprised to find that it was divided into small centres like farms, each yard with its crumbling, peeling and miserable farmhouse, as all Italian farmhouses were at that time. Donna Lydia explained to me that this was Federico's 'great idea'—to keep the mares and yearlings in small, isolated groups so that there should be no contact in the event of an epidemic. I do not think plans were ever made to do up or repair those wretched houses. The truth is that Tesio's means had always been limited and whatever he had he spent on acquiring land or mares. The area was already overpopulated and he would buy any piece of land large enough and flat enough to make paddocks.

It was amusing to hear him tell why he had chosen Dormello—it had very little to do with horses! His grandmother had had a villa and a beautiful estate in Brianza and had always said that she would bequeath it to him so that he could live there and breed horses. Tesio sold the property as soon as his grandmother died. Intuition told him that good horses could not be raised in Brianza and the fate of other studs in the region have proved him right. He started to search for a piece of land which would suit him and eventually selected Dormello because 'the atmosphere's damp and the ground's dry.' The soil is light and permeable and, even if Arona does not quite deserve the bad reputation for damp attributed to Como, it comes close to it. This was a good reason. Another was that 'the soil of Dormello is part of the glacial moraine system of Monte Rosa, the largest on the slopes of the Southern Alps, and the moraines, especially those of Monte Rosa, contain every imaginable natural element—including gold'. Tesio never mentioned of what use gold might be in the nutrition of young horses!

There may have been gold but there was not a trace of calcium in the Dormello soil. It has always been universally accepted that calcareous grazing ground produces good bone structure in horses but Tesio maintained that calcium was unnecessary: 'Animals create calcium from other elements. Who would deny that the ibex and chamois of the Gran Paradiso have excellent bone structures? And yet the Gran Paradiso is formed entirely of igneous rock without the slightest trace of calcium.' I confess that I never dared to confute this theory because I never took the trouble to study a geological map of the

Gran Paradiso. But, today, in the light of present scientific knowledge, it may no longer be a heresy to maintain that one element can be transformed into another—so maybe it was not so ridiculous to believe that animals are able to 'create' calcium.

Tesio's most recent purchase at Dormello had been a piece of land known as 'La Surga', situated on the top of a hill. Cavaliere d'Arpino was among the first batch of yearlings to graze these paddocks where horses had never browsed before. Four years earlier Apelle, too, had been reared on new ground which had previously been a peasant smallholding used for the cultivation of maize and potatoes and which, earlier still, had been a wood. Tesio believed firmly in the strength of new land: 'Even a courtyard will do, provided horses have never been raised there before.'

At the time of my first visit to Dormello there was a yearling at La Surga named Jacopa del Sellaio. She was the object of great attention as she was a daughter of Coronach. It was the period when the line of Matchem and West Australian seemed as if it would gain advantage over the stock descended from Eclipse and Herod—with the successes of Hurry On, Captain Cuttle, Coronach and Call Boy. Coronach was the finest representative of this line and it had been a considerable financial effort for Tesio to send Jacopa's dam to visit him. Now Jacopa was at La Surga, rather thin and light of bone, she had white stockings, a blaze down her face, and prominent rather wild eyes but Donna Lydia, who took us to see her, admired her greatly and her praises were echoed, dutifully, by the stud groom who accompanied us.

Jacopa was said to be a 'magnificent filly' but her feet were causing some anxiety: they were large, broad feet with low soles. Her dam, Viceversa, was thin soled and her feet had caused trouble. Did Jacopa's feet have thin soles? Tesio decided not: flat feet, yes, lowered soles, yes, and thin walls which could make shoeing a problem—but not thin soles! This was one of the many examples of wishful thinking which enabled Tesio to act on a decision made against all the evidence. On this occasion it worked and Jacopa's feet caused no trouble.

CHAPTER 2

First visit to Newmarket: Partnership

I DID NOT go back to Dormello that year—Bolgheri, the home of my fiancée, had become more important to me and our marriage was to take place in October the following year.

Country weddings have an atmosphere which city weddings cannot have and Bolgheri on the 18th October, 1930, had that of a country festival. Festoons of ivy and foliage decorated the scene; farmers and gamekeepers were in their Sunday best. There was applause, endless handshakes, open air refreshments, champagne and gaiety.

Naturally the Tesios were also invited—but here there is a lapse in my memory. Whereas I recall perfectly the radiant presence of Donna Lydia, I cannot remember if Tesio himself was there.

After October 18th there was a brief period during which I saw neither horses, racecourses, nor Tesio; six weeks to be precise—because, at the end of November, my wife and I joined the Tesios at Newmarket to buy our first horses at the December Sales. When I was a child, already fascinated by horses, my father had described Newmarket and its great sales to me, conjuring up visions of magnificent horses. Those images had remained impressed in my mind for a long time and had returned when I heard Donna Lydia speak of Newmarket, as a Mutaw-wif would speak of Mecca. The Tesios attended the sales each year.

The accommodation at the December Sales in 1930 did not correspond in any way with my childhood dreams, nor with Donna Lydia's enthusiastic descriptions. How different it was from the centrally-heated and upholstered environment where Tatersalls hold their sales today! A flimsy roof afforded less than adequate protection from the arctic conditions to clients and spectators alike. A bed of straw protected our feet. Only a select few (I never knew how they came to be selected) sat in the comparative warmth of a box-like construction at the foot of the auctioneer's rostrum. In the bitter cold the assembled experts and enthusiasts presented a strange sight to our inexperienced eyes. Their clothes were the most curious assortment of greasy collared mackintoshes, ancient sheepskin jackets, antediluvian overcoats—dirty and worn, fur hats, felt hats with woollen scarves tied over or underneath them, hobnailed boots, hunting boots, wellingtons, fur boots, moth-eaten woollen gloves. In their search for protection from the biting weather the gathering resembled a tramps' convention rather than the élite of the racing world enjoying one of the highlights of the year.

My wife and I knew and were known by no one. The Tesios knew and were known by every one; every one, that is, who was worth knowing—but their greetings were always fleeting, their meetings hasty and all conversation reduced to a minimum.

In Italy, if you meet an acquaintance at the races (or at a funeral), you are drawn into endless futile conversations. In England people go to the races to bet, to see the horses, or both. They go to the sales to buy or to sell. Absorbed by their own affairs they bother their neighbours as little as possible—so as not to be bothered by them.

As we waited one each side of Donna Lydia for the fateful moment when the first of our lot numbers would enter the ring, in the midst of the milling crowd it was as though we were alone. No one, not even Donna Lydia's friends, came near us. Tesio was on his own, standing somewhere among the throng concentrating, as always, on the horses and studying his catalogue which was filled with notes and comments. My wife and I had asked Donna Lydia to seek Tesio's advice on our behalf, having decided to buy some horses to race in our own name and colours. Having studied the catalogue he sent the reply via Donna Lydia that the animals we should buy were two two-year-old fillies named Polka and Joan Lowell. I was overcome with excitement when the bidding started and, in my enthusiasm, bid several times against myself—much to the amusement of the onlookers.

The two fillies cost me less than a thousand guineas— though I must have spent almost as much again at Gilbert's, the famous saddlers, buying colours, rugs, saddles and bridles for them.

Both fillies enjoyed particularly undistinguished racing careers. Joan Lowell had won a small race in England as a two-year-old but, in her new career in Italy, she ran three times unplaced and was retired to the stud. Polka ran several times as a three-year-old, eventually managing to win her last race of the season. The following year she won her first race and was sold. To this day I have never understood why we sold Polka and kept Joan Lowell. During her stud career the latter produced Gabbro, who was to be Nearco's inseparable work companion, and Grumolo who was, in turn, assigned to the same humble but useful function for Niccolò dell 'Arca. Both these horses were exceptionally tough and sound—which was essential to enable them to stand up to their work partners and to Tesio's training methods. Thanks to these two lead horses, Joan Lowell was admitted to the olympus of Dormello and her blood runs there still among her descendants at Dormello-Olgiata.

A full year had passed since our expedition to Newmarket. We had changed trainers three times and our enthusiasm diminished with each disappointment. We were not thinking of making further purchases although we continued the futile careers of our two fillies. But we often went racing at Pisa and were always welcomed by Donna Lydia on our frequent visits to the Hotel Nettuno. It was during one of these visits that Tesio asked us, through our patroness, if we would like to become their partners in the stud and racing stable. Had our own venture been more successful maybe we would have been reluctant to give up the idea of one day having a stable of our own, with our own colours. However, since our failure had been dismal, the alternative now offered was all the more attractive. The price was, for the time, colossal, but the situation was unique so could not be discussed on the basis of any precedent. The decision depended on whether we could pay the sum asked. We were able to do so and the deal was concluded *ipso facto.*

I cannot recall having signed a contract nor any piece of paper, nor having received any such signed by Tesio—nor do I remember the date of the agreement. But I remember that one day, in the spring of 1932, the horses which had previously run in the name of Federico Tesio appeared on the race cards as being the property of 'Tesio-Incisa'. Less than three weeks later it was my wife who led in Jacopa del Sellaio after her victory in the Italian Derby.

Our association with Tesio did not in any way alter the running of the stud or the racing stable. As always, I was welcomed with open arms by Donna Lydia and now with a new warmth by Tesio, but the presence of the 'Lady' of Dormello was too dominant and that of the 'Lord' of the stables too awesome for any intrusion of mine to be even thinkable. This reserve, which lasted for the duration of our partnership with the Tesios, spared me from an unpleasant humiliation. I honestly believed that I was associated with the entire Tesio complex. It was only many years later, at the time the deed for the 'Società per Azioni Razza Dormello-Olgiata' was drawn up, I learned from my lawyer that, until then, we had possessed *only a share of the horses*. Nothing else—not even the head collars to take them away had Tesio told me to get out!

Upon the formation of the company my wife and I became shareholders, not only in the horses but in the land, buildings, deadstock and even the head collars! But the fact that for over twenty years I had fully believed myself to have rights and properties which I did not have, shows how successful our 'gentleman's agreement' had been. Above all it proves the delicacy and discretion of the Tesios who never once let us suspect that our position was in any way inferior to theirs.

Our early arrangement also suited Tesio well for, in our partnership, he found no element of competition. In his early youth he had been a reckless gambler (écarté and baccarat). He had not touched a card since, deciding to devote himself to horses, but he had retained that youthful aggression which kept him constantly on the alert for possible rivals, (to be struck down instantly before they could retaliate). He never ceased to delight in competition and any successful deal was for him incomparably entertaining.

To Tesio, anyone who raced for love of the game or for amusement was a fool; there were a hundred more interesting and enticing pastimes. Thoroughbreds should be kept to win races, to beat others and take the prizes.

When on one occasion he was advised not to keep all his eggs in one basket, to invest at least some of his gains in shares, he replied: 'Certainly not! I have no reason to believe that Pirelli makes tyres or Agnelli cars any better than I make horses.'

CHAPTER 3

Early recollections and marriage

I KNOW VERY little about Tesio other than what I learned directly from him during the twenty-two years of our association. He mentioned his grandmother but only in connection with the villa in Brianza. I know that his father, who was Piedmontese, died when he was three or four years old. I know even less about his mother, who must have died shortly afterwards, and nothing at all about the guardian who sent him to a boarding school at Moncalieri when he was orphaned.

His recollections of his many years at Moncalieri (perhaps the best school in Italy), were few and fragmentary but he liked to tell how when he presented himself, ill prepared, for his examinations, he would fix the teacher with a steely gaze and say to himself: 'Look out or I will kill you. If you do not pass me you will die. Fail me and I will kill you!' This, he affirmed, was how he passed his exams. I do not know if his hypnotic powers were as decisive as he claimed but I did discover that he excelled in all his scholastic work and was proclaimed, as was then the custom, 'Emperor of Studies'. He never boasted of this and claimed that he had never re-entered the place once his schooling was completed. 'Thirteen years was enough!' he would say with a certain Piedmontese twist brought back by the memory.

His recollections of Moncalieri were not unhappy and

he once said: 'If you know the rules and they do not change, you can adapt to them. In the end you feel freer than if they were constantly changing, even if it were for the better.'

The regulations at Moncalieri were unchanging. Each pupil had his own room where he enjoyed complete privacy and freedom outside school hours. In the evening the door was locked from the outside and the single candle had to be blown out at a given hour. This was checked through a spy-hole in the door. It was in the privacy of his room, which became for him a studio, that Tesio started to paint with a passion which was to last throughout his life.

Tesio was inordinately proud of the fact that, from the day he entered the school at the age of six until the day he left, he never once drank water at a meal. The wine was Trani and Barletta, strong, popular Italian wines which could be cut with a knife. Each boy had a daily ration—a quarter litre with each meal. Many of the pupils were unable to drink it and passed their rations to Tesio—who would accept them with gusto!

Tesio's science master was a Barnabite Father named Francesco Denza who was later to become renowned as Director of the Vatican Observatory. Tesio claimed to have been one of Denza's favourite pupils and of having long and fascinating conversations with him during which he was taught a great deal about meteorology. His knowledge of this subject must have evaporated with the passing years for, in later life, Tesio's idea of atmospheric phenomena was restricted to the notion that it must not rain on the day of a race for which he had a runner!

Another of Tesio's reminiscences I will attempt to recount—with discretion! The young Princess Laetitia Bonaparte, a buxom young beauty some three years older than Tesio (twelve at the time), lived in the royal castle at

Moncalieri. A niece of Napoleon and of Victor Emanuel II, this young beauty attended certain classes at the college. She sat in the front row within sight of all the other children and was passionately admired by Tesio. A school orchestra had been formed and it was compulsory for all pupils to join. Each child was allowed to choose the instrument he wished to play and Tesio had selected the clarinet. Music was not amongst his many talents. But his clarinet did not go unappreciated. In the darkness and privacy of his room, with the vivid imagination of the very young, it became a substitute for the delectable, but unobtainable, Princess Laetitia.

When Tesio left college at the age of nineteen, his guardian handed him 500,000 lire (in 1898 equivalent to £20,000 *gold*, an enormous sum in those days), which had been left to him by his parents, and told him to go and do as he pleased with the money. This extraordinarily irresponsible guardian never concerned himself with Tesio's welfare again.

Tesio gave amusing accounts of his introduction into worldly society shortly after leaving the college at Moncalieri. At that time, when wives had to appear virtuous and husbands, for honour's sake, jealous, there was a well defined class of women whose manners were very distinguished—even if their morals were not. They were known as *demi-mondaines*—I never understood why for they were, of course, *entirely* worldly. Unlike the women of the Viale Majno in Milan or those who warm themselves by braziers on the Viale di Tor di Quinto (the fires are lit in order to attract customers), the *demi-mondaines* had beautiful houses, elegant carriages and pairs, and sumptuous jewels.

Tesio was encouraged by some friends, older and more experienced than he, to visit one such lady. He had met her a few days earlier and, although strongly attracted, he had not found the courage to approach her. His friends assured him that he need have no apprehensions—the lady was willing! Tesio set off to visit her with due regard for custom: the time was three o'clock in the afternoon (four-thirty being the hour at which ladies left their houses for their daily carriage ride when they would trot smartly up and down the Corso in Rome or round and round the Piazza d'Armi in Turin), a frock coat was worn, top hat, gloves and a cane to complete the outfit. Manners required that the drawing room should be reached with this regalia intact.

The lady, in a cloud of veils and lace, lay languidly on a chaise-longue: the young Tesio's visit had been announced.

'What a pleasure to see you! Bring up a chair and come and sit next to me. Forgive me for stretching out like this—I am so tired.' Tesio did not have to be asked twice. He pulled up a chair, put his gloves inside his hat and the hat under his chair, sat down and, since his friends had exhorted him to be unembarrassed, immediately began to make unambiguous preparations for the activities which were the purpose of his visit.

These preparations in a frock coat which, as I mentioned, was double-breasted, must have been somewhat complicated and laborious—particularly while he remained seated. The belle, however, perhaps absorbed in rosy dreams of her wooer about to start a passionate scene, did not appear to notice. When his sartorial adjustments were completed, Tesio took her abandoned hand and made all too clear the motives for his visit. He instantly received the most resounding slap of his life!

This was the only gallant adventure of which Tesio ever spoke to me. I think that the experience served for the rest of his life—it also taught him to beware of the advice of friends. Perhaps this was the reason he never listened to anyone! Everything he did hereafter—he did his own way.

After completing his military service as a second lieutenant in the cavalry, Tesio took a diplomatic course at the University in Florence and I think that it must have been at this point that he became a close friend of his future brother-in-law, Stefano Flori. Both were compulsive gamblers. I do not know which was the ringleader in this passion but Flori had a very wealthy father and Tesio had his 500,000 lire in cash, so both were in a position to gamble—and to lose. While still young, both became members of the exclusive club, the Circolo della Caccia. Flori owned racehorses and had won the Italian Derby in 1899. Tesio, although not yet an owner, rode chasing and on the flat for Flori and other friends. It seems he was not a good rider but, what he lacked in style, he more than made up for in courage and dash and was undeterred by the terrifying falls and injuries he sustained.

When eventually he stopped riding, Tesio also stopped gambling and never did so again. At about the same time he married Lydia Flori, the younger of Stefano's two sisters, and together they started the stud and racing stable which were to have such a profound and lasting effect on the thoroughbred stud-book. The Dormello colours of white with scarlet cross-belts and cap were chosen in a rather haphazard way during a visit to the races, the colours of the first winner of the day being combined with those of the winner of the second race.

Tesio decided to breed and train his horses himself. He was convinced that if the work was undertaken in a professional manner, even a fool would be able to beat the horses of that era whose gentleman owners were non-professional and amateurs. He knew that *he* was not a fool.

All that Tesio achieved was possible because Donna Lydia was there to help him. The brilliance was his, all his and only his—but to enable him to develop his ideas, his inventions, and his discoveries, it was essential that someone should do the humble chores and settle all the petty and often ridiculous problems which, surprisingly, would baffle him completely. This had to be done selflessly: if Donna Lydia expressed an idea of her own Tesio would either ignore it completely or, if it was a good one, adopt it as being one of his own. Nevertheless, from the beginning of their marriage through the many years which followed, Tesio's behaviour towards Donna Lydia was exemplary. He responded to her profound admiration and to her docile and undiscriminating worship with affectionate deference and the kindest attentions.

But it is certain that he took no account of Donna Lydia's opinions concerning matings. This area was completely his and he would brook no interference—even though he had to all intents and purposes delegated to her the actual running of the stud. He trusted her completely to interpret and carry out his instructions at Dormello. Surrounded, as he felt himself to be, by hostility and bearers of ill fortune, his wife was the only person in whose loyalty he had complete confidence. Donna Lydia was an indispensable complement to Tesio. Her character was diametrically opposed to his—as were her ways, her upbringing and her education. She would shower the horses with manifestations of affections as though they were people (shocking her very Catholic sister who regarded this attitude as blasphemous), whereas Tesio definitely did not share her fondness for them. He knew how to judge, understand, and interpret their individual characters and he respected them. 'Leave him alone,' he would constantly say, perhaps applying to the horse what he would have wished for himself.

On occasion Tesio would even defend the horses against Donna Lydia's excesses of affection: 'It is not necessary to go into the paddocks all the time to see the horses. How would you like it if, while you were eating, someone were to put his foot right into your plate of spaghetti? Grass is what they eat; why trample all over it?' Donna Lydia never fully appreciated the connection between grass and spaghetti and even Tesio's repeated exhortations to 'leave them alone' made no impression on her. Yet she was invaluable to him in countless ways: as his secretary and, prior to our association, as his accountant. Her bookkeeping, whilst somewhat primitive, was also effective. In a notebook she would fill in the expenditures on one page: 'paid nomination to Gainsborough, so much, bought three stamps, so much'. On the opposite page the receipts: 'sold mare in foal to Hurry On, so much, sold an old rig to the rag-pickers, so much'. Every lira was accounted for in her little book. Sometimes, too, she had to act as a 'nanny' to him—telling him whether or not he should take a raincoat or an umbrella—and she always had to fill his fountain pen for him as he was quite incapable of doing so without covering his hands and clothes with ink!

If Tesio was travelling abroad and, say, stopping in Paris on his way to England, Donna Lydia would put francs in one of his pockets, sterling in another, and his passport in a third. On one trip to Paris she gave him a large cheque to take to the Société d'Encouragement and a letter to deliver by hand to a friend. Despite all her meticulous precautions, he gave the cheque (without any envelope or directions), to the hall porter of his hotel and, after an absence of ten days, returned with the letter to Donna Lydia's friend still in his pocket.

CHAPTER 4

The personality of Tesio

TESIO UNDOUBTEDLY HAD good manners. Since he
had never known his parents and his guardian had been
completely indifferent to him, this behaviour must have
been the result of school teaching, (at that time manners
were still taught), and would have been further refined
and polished by the fellow officers of his regiment, the
future diplomats with whom he had studied in Florence,
and by the members of the Roman club, the Circolo della
Caccia. At the same time he would react to any
provocation or injustice with the rapidity of a cobra whose
tail has been trampled. This may have been due to the fact
that he belonged to a generation which was very conscious
of its social position—or simply to his determined and
spirited character.

Tesio had a strong personality; he was totally lacking
in sentimentality but I believe that he was fundamentally
and genuinely good. Sentimentality is so often intended to
appear good, and quickly becomes mawkish. Tesio was
the very opposite of this. Not in the least concerned with
appearances, he was one of the few people (or should I say
Italians?) who applied literally the evangelical precept:
'Let your communication be, Yea, yea; Nay, nay.'

He said what he meant and his orders were clear,
precise, and final. He left no escape for himself should
these orders prove to result in error or failure. The ability

to impose complete, passive obedience on all those under his jurisdiction was combined with a severe intolerance of any mistake, carelessness or stupidity on their part.

To those who did not have the opportunity, as I so often did, to see there there was no trace of malice in his outbursts of impatience, this lack of compassion might have seemed a negative side to Tesio's character. These outbursts were due to the severity which he applied systematically to himself—he would punish himself by fasting, giving up cigarettes or some other innocent pleasure if, for example, he had overworked a horse or a race had been lost without good reason. Severity was applied to all those who worked for or with him but, once the penalty was paid, the episode was forgotten without rancour or further recriminations.

Many considered him to be a selfish man. This was not so. It was an impression created by his total and inflexible dedication to the task to which he had devoted his life. He was stubbornly single-minded, not egocentric. The following episode typifies this single-mindedness. A cloud-burst had caused catastrophic flooding throughout southern Italy and had severed roads and railways. On the day following, Tesio managed to arrange an appointment with a government minister who, he hoped, would intervene on our behalf so that one of our horses could travel to Naples for a race. The minister explained that this was absolutely impossible. Every available means of transport was being used for rescue work. Tesio's reply was: 'But I *must* run in the Gran Premio.' 'I *must*' not 'I wish to.' This conviction that to run a horse was a duty, a moral obligation, distinguished Tesio from all other owners. It was not presumption, of which he was fre-quently accused, but his belief in the value of his work. At the time such reactions seemed absurd but the years have given a different perspective and, in the light of the results he achieved and their lasting effects, his single-mindedness appears perfectly acceptable.

Generosity was not a characteristic of the Tesios. Tesio himself would never refuse what was just and would never dispute a financial obligation—but he believed it immoral to give or concede anything for nothing. Donna Lydia, on the other hand, considered it a matter of conscience to bargain over everything. She was an arch traditionalist and felt duty bound to administer by governing, with the consequent right to adjust the compensation according to the zeal with which her orders had been carried out.

Tesio would regale us with most amusing stories of his improbable adventures—new and different every time. At an early point in his career he had travelled widely. Rumour had it that the reason behind his departure on these first travels was an unsuccessful attempt on the virtue of a married woman. It happened at the Hotel Nettuno in Pisa. He had conceived the insane idea of trying to seduce the lady by entering her bedroom through the window. It seems that his ejection, by the same route, was instantaneous. Whether from anger or shame (far be it from me to suspect that it was from fear of her husband), Tesio left Pisa at dawn the following morning and set out on his journey round the world.

He would tell how Chinese barbers would shave the entire face from one ear to the other with a single terrifying stroke of the razor; how he had ridden in a race on a Chinese pony (sometimes, though not always, he said he had won the Peking Derby); how, having been invited several times by the most important mandarins of the Celestial Empire, he had seen the sober but very elegant décor of their houses changed for each visit—yet another exquisite vase with another single beautiful flower, another rare carpet or beautiful piece of furniture. He found the Japanese coarse by comparison: 'But they too have better taste than us—small houses with a few beautiful things; not these dreadful buildings of ours crammed from floor to ceiling with oddments from every epoch! And then we enter with our shoes on!' (This reflection did not persuade him to change his habit of wearing in the house, the same shoes in which he had just been round the stables in Milan!)

Then there were tales of his travels in Argentina when he rode from Buenos Aires to Patagonia alone, followed by his *tropilla* from which, now and again, he would take and saddle a horse when the one he was riding was tired. And how all the *tropilla* would lie on the ground when the *pampèro* was about to blow. The horses would sense its arrival when the air was still completely calm, long before he did. During the very long journey the only human he encountered was a German shepherd with his flock. He had not seen a live soul for years and survived on lambs' meat alone. (Tesio had worked out how long the German would be able to live, bearing in mind the fact that each of his ewes would average one lamb a year and that the German, who only ate the tastiest morsels, ate one lamb every two days.)

Tesio believed that everyone could be taken in by his improvised yarns—many of which were utter nonsense. He would hold forth, too, about an alleged discovery of his—going into the most minute details—whereas, in fact, it was something well-known. He would reveal as personal inventions, inventions made by others long before. This ingenuousness was probably due to the fact that Tesio had spent so many years mainly in the company of lads who, probably out of deference, listened to him without turning a hair.

Taxation of stables, as viewed by the Italian Revenue, was a subject which Tesio regarded with a childlike simplicity. He would state with absolute conviction that: 'A racing stable is not taxable. When a horse becames lame it loses its value. Since, in theory, all the horses could become lame at the same time, the worth of a stable is nil'—a view shared by the British tax authorities. Although he would argue this point with great conviction, Tesio would never, unlike the vast majority of Italians, have resorted to subterfuge or trickery to avoid paying the taxes in question.

Tesio considered sleep to be a waste of time. The recommended eight hours of sleep shortened a man's life by a third; it also accounted for much of the foolishness of the young. One could not have great expectations of a twenty-one year old who, having spent one third of his life asleep, had only fourteen years' experience behind him! He himself was able to sleep at any time, for ten minutes or two hours, whenever he had nothing to do, to speak about, or to listen to, or whenever a subject under discussion was of no interest to him—regardless of the participants.

He always slept whilst travelling, using hours which would have been wasted in any case. At home he slept only in snatches. In his room at Dormello he had two beds—one on which to sleep—the other for the books he would read during the night. I say 'read' but he was not a methodical reader. He used books primarily for reference, to resolve some problem or to satisfy his insatiable curiosity in every field of knowledge. There were books on every subject—biographies, history, history of art, veterinary science, medicine, botany—and novels and detective stories for distraction and relaxation. Crossword puzzles were another distraction from his daily preoccupations and, although he no longer ever played a serious game of cards, he would occasionally feel like a game of backgammon. Not a serious game, requiring little concentration. A game for which Tesio required an adversary not quite his match. On these occasions he called on Donna Lydia who always, obligingly, lost with good grace.

His daily rounds of strenuous activity were the more remarkable as Tesio did not enjoy particularly good health. He frequently suffered from minor ailments; his eyes and teeth troubled him and he was prone to colds and violent coughs which he found difficult to shake off— being constantly exposed to the cold and damp autumnal and winter mornings. He would be smitten with sudden and violent stomach or intestinal complaints, probably caused by his incorrigibly erratic eating habits but, when he complained—giving horrifying descriptions intended especially for Donna Lydia—he always maintained that he had no time to take care of himself.

CHAPTER 5

Painting and furniture making

ALTHOUGH TESIO'S CHOSEN profession kept him in close contact with the most frivolous and philistine category of Italian society, his own cultural level was exceptionally high. He had studied the classics at Moncalieri and taken a degree in Florence—his childhood and youth were spent in surroundings where culture was naturally absorbed.

I think, however, that he was completely lacking in musical talent, in spite of his early discovery of the unsuspected merits of the clarinet! As a young man he must have been to the opera. It amused him to quote some of the more ridiculous rhetoric from arias or duets but I never heard him hum or whistle a theme from an opera, nor did he go to concerts or listen to classical music on the radio. Despite his familiarity with literature, Tesio was not appreciative of the theatre, with the exception of French comedies, *pochades*. These he would visit when in Paris.

Horses were his profession, his concern for them an over-riding necessity, but painting was his great love, the true passion of his life.

Tesio painted throughout his life, from earliest youth into old age. He experimented with every technique from oils to frescos, water colour to pastel, and became very learned in the history of art, going frequently to museums, galleries, and exhibitions in Italy and elsewhere.

It was during a visit to London that I realised the extent of Tesio's enjoyment of art. Together we visited the Royal Academy to see an exhibition of paintings and sculpture from the Royal Collection. Tesio was entranced, overcome with excitement. He studied, analysed, and commented on each work. He led me to look closely at the hand of an old man in a picture by Rembrandt. 'Just look, see how it's painted! Two strokes of pure colour here, a touch of another colour there. All pure colours put on without any hesitation! A shade of green here and the red there ... Now stand back and look at it. Do you see the blood circulating? Do you see? It's alive!'

Tesio was particularly intrigued by the techniques of art and had a strong sense of colour. He could remember particular colours with astonishing accuracy. If Donna Lydia required a length of material she had only to show him a sample cutting. He would glance briefly at it and was then able to buy a perfect match in Milan. He told me that, when painting, he never felt as sure of the design as he did of the colour. For him colour, light, and depth, predominated over form. Perhaps this is why Tesio's pictures of horses, a subject so familiar to him, appear rather incongruous and disconcerting.

Tesio painted the official portrait of Torbido for the Italian Jockey Club collection. He disliked the traditional static pose so often used for such pictures—the jockey in the saddle, an emerald-green track, dazzling white rails, a cobalt blue sky ... When he painted Torbido he showed him in profile on the shores of Lake Maggiore. Rocca d'Angera is in the background, a bare tree is bent by the wind, the sky is dark and *turbid*, threatening a *storm*. This symbolised the horse's name and that of his dam,

Tempesta, but such subtlety was little appreciated by the Italian Jockey Club. Many years passed before coloured lithographs of the picture were printed and put on sale. Perhaps the lack of enthusiasm on the part of the Jockey Club was justified, for the Torbido lithograph is in less demand than any of the ninety others still available today.

The formula adopted by Tesio for his portrait of Tenerani was even more original. The horse is riderless and without saddle or bridle. His jockey stands in front of him. In the background is a thick wood while in the lower right-hand corner there is a miniature of a scene from the 1947 Gran Premio Milano race, which was run in a downpour. The picture of Torbido was eventually and reluctantly accepted but that of Tenerani ended up in a back room at Dormello and is reproduced here for the first time.

Also illustrated are two pastels: the bust of a child leaning out of a window was executed in 1882 when Tesio was thirteen years old. The other shows an old man uncorking a bottle—a drawing made by Tesio two years later when he was fifteen.

I have never been able to discover when or how Tesio set up his furniture factory. However, it is a fact that at some period he was involved in interior decoration. The interior of Dormello was almost entirely furnished with pieces conceived, designed and manufactured in his workshop and was inspired by the Art Nouveau which was in fashion at the time. Even the metal, wood, and ceramic, handles and fittings for each individual piece were modelled in plasticine by him before being carved, shaped, or cast in the final materials.

Art Nouveau enjoyed only a short period of popularity and was soon scoffed at, and later condemned, as a perversion of taste. (A friend of Tesio's once confided earnestly to me: 'Thank heaven Federico stopped making furniture and started making horses!') Fifty years later furniture, lampshades, paper-cutters, ash-trays, and flower vases of the Art Nouveau style rose giddily in price and found a ready and enthusiastic market.

A few years ago I was asked to lend a chair from Dormello, designed by Tesio and made in his workshop, to an exhibition on the early twentieth century which was being held at the Poldi Pezzoli Museum. It was gazed at with reverence and greatly admired by connoisseurs. When the exhibition came to an end I was offered an enormous sum for it (a million lire, 1972), by a collector who wished to acquire it at all costs. Comparing the cost of the manufacture of the chair and the outlay involved in producing a (probably useless) racehorse, I could not but wonder if Tesio did well to give up his workshop in favour of his stable.

Tesio's interest in the arts and letters, his attempt, only so recently appreciated, to maintain an artistic level in furniture making (which was by then already becoming mechanised), his continuous and tireless research and experiments with his horses, all stemmed from the insatiable, youthful curiosity which enabled him to retain his extraordinary vitality throughout his long life.

The ability to synthesise, the essence of human intellect, was manifest in Tesio. His deductions were immediate— as were the decisions he drew from them. He believed that decisions should be made instinctively, not through reasoning, and held that the world changes more rapidly than our senses perceive so that any assumption based on precedent is, by definition, outdated. In the end this conviction prevailed over him to such an extent that it seemed to him pernicious to reflect before making up his mind on any point.

Of course he *thought* that he took decisions without thinking because he did not have to think about them at that instant, but his instinctive actions were the product of *years* of intense and, at times, tormenting uncertainty and deep thought. The truth was that he did not think about a problem when a decision was necessary, he had thought about such problems all his life.

To justify this supposed "acting on instinct', Tesio would cite Julius Caesar as an example. Always a great admirer of Caesar, Tesio would eulogise about him in a curious and unexpected way: 'Caesar was short' (this no doubt due to an old complex of Tesio's), 'but he had the energy of a hundred men! He did not speak much but he acted. How he acted! Cicero was large and pompous with a thundering baritone voice but, in front of Caesar he quailed and trembled like a leaf.' It wasn't just the fact that Caesar could make Cicero tremble which fascinated Tesio. It was because the dictator's military and political successes were due to the lightning rapidity of his decisions.

Is this historically correct? Tesio often repeated the incident, evidently amused as though it was he who had reduced Cicero to his quivering state. In his heart of hearts I think that his 'Cicero's' were the pompous gentlemen of the Circolo della Caccia and the Italian Jockey Club who, in the early days, had openly laughed at him when he said that one day he would win the Grand Prix de Paris.

This attitude among the hierarchy of Italian flat-racing endured throughout Tesio's remarkable career. They were incapable of understanding his ideas or following his arguments and barricaded themselves behind a wall of obstinate and senseless opposition inspired by ignorant mistrust: 'If Tesio says it, it is because it suits Tesio.' They never understood that Tesio had no time for duplicity or intrigue. He was too busy to unravel the subterfuges of others and, in any case, he did not have a suspicious nature. Tesio's originality stemmed from his intellectual isolation. This, combined with brilliant intelligence made his conversation lively and altogether delightful.

Tesio never held a position of authority in the administration of racing. His intelligence, clear-sightedness and experience were ignored, despised, and discredited. Consequently Italian flat-racing sank to an abysmal standard; Tesio thrived in the sport at an international level.

It must, however, be said, that Tesio did not attempt to understand the administration's way of thinking either. He neglected completely to study his fellow men before whom he remained in many ways still a child at the age of eighty. Perhaps if he had shown more consideration, they would have been less cold in their dealings with him.

CHAPTER 6

The superstitions and 'science' of Tesio

PEOPLE DO NOT become superstitious; they are born so. Tesio's legendary capacity for superstition increased with the years. Each minor mishap appeared to relate to a previous incident and, when this re-occurred, he believed the relevant sequel would follow.

According to Tesio friars brought bad luck because 'they wear patience.' Who knows today that, in Italy, the scapular worn by certain orders of friars was called '*pazienza*'? Tesio's prejudice in this case came from the curious reasoning that 'patience' can mean resignation and endurance and is, therefore, associated with adversity. Priests did not bring misfortune since they did not wear 'patience'.

Cats, whatever their colour, brought bad luck if they crossed your path: it was less harmful if from left to right, more so if from right to left, and *very* bad if the cat was black. It would then be necessary to stop and 'have the street cleaned' by someone else. I was never sure whether it had to be someone going in the same direction or whether it worked equally well from the opposite direction. When there was not much traffic the possibility that someone else would come and 'clean' was unlikely and the delay could last quite a while. If, on the other hand, there was a great deal of traffic, the situation was quickly remedied—but the sudden halt, however brief, meant that all the cars behind had to halt too—causing a cacophony of angry honks and toots which Tesio's driver was instructed to ignore.

It was common knowledge on every racecourse that it was an anathema to wish Tesio luck for a race. Nevertheless, from time to time an ingenuous 'well-wisher' (or perhaps, more rarely, a 'mischief-maker'), risked bidding him good luck. All hell would then break loose! All the most effective and well tried exorcisms had to be called out immediately. Unfortunately these were also the most ostentatious and spectacular. I remember at Mirabello, when Ugolino da Siena was running in his first big race, a kindly and distinguished gentleman said: 'All the best, Commendatore.' Tesio immediately gasped: 'I'm done for!' Five minutes later his exorcisms failed—Ugolino was shamefully defeated.

Obviously it was extremely dangerous for thirteen to be seated at table. Only once did this happen to Tesio. One of the thirteen was a priest who assured those present that there was not the slightest risk. To Tesio these assurances were futile and he was on tenter-hooks throughout the meal. The following day the priest died ... 'Luckily,' said Tesio, 'he settled the matter quickly.'

The 13th too had sinister connotations, but the 17th brought luck. Tesio's birthday was on January 17th, which is the feast of St. Anthony, in Italy a traditional protector of domestic animals, and Tesio assumed that it was the Saint who had consecrated him to horses.

To stumble over a threshold or a stone, particularly before a race, was a hitch. It was a warning, not a complete disaster. If he went back a few steps and waved the foot which had tripped, backwards and forwards over the obstacle (if it was solid) the road to success would be reopened; if the obstacle was mobile, such as a loose stone, he had to get it out of the way with a stroke of his stick, used as a golf club. The astonished public would watch these manoeuvres without a clue as to their significance.

Every superstition had an origin, a purpose and an antidote: for example—you should never accept money (*never*, neither a payment, a repayment, nor even as a share of a Dutch treat in a restaurant) immediately before a race. Fortune, seeing that there have already been takings, might consider that nothing further was necessary and you would be deprived of the prize.

Nor should you drink before a race in which you have a runner. You should drink after a victory, not before, otherwise it could appear that your horse had already won and the fates would not give their indispensable assistance.

You should not drink coffee before a race. Here the explanation was more obscure. Tesio feared that the coffee might be accidentally spilled and this was as disastrous as spilling salt. Coffee is black and Tesio had an obsession about black. Black is sad, black is death, black is nothingness. As a logical consequence Tesio never admitted to having a black horse—they were brown—and woe betide anyone who said they were black!

As for salt, a burning defeat, a few hours after a salt-cellar had been upset, had confirmed Tesio's convictions on the subject of bad luck, evil eye and sorcery. It was at Maxim's on the day of the Grand Prix de Paris, 1937. The Tesios and I were there lunching together. In laying the table the waiter knocked over the salt-cellar and the entire contents spilled onto the table-cloth.

'We're beaten!' said Tesio with complete calm and, for once, without getting upset. ... Three hours later, Donatello suffered the first defeat of his career.

Tesio hated to be photographed. He was convinced that, if the picture fell into the hands of an adversary, it would be used to malicious ends—(for example to stick pins in his eyes, etc.) to make him lose races.

Sometimes he would act rashly for obscure reasons. Nobody understood why but, one day, Ghislanda appeared almost dock-tailed to take part in a race at San Siro. Tesio himself had cut her previously abundant tail. He explained that she had been given too much weight in the race and, this way, she would carry three or four pounds less. But this excuse was an absolute contradiction of his usual theory that there is an extraordinary reserve of strength in hair. 'Man is stronger than woman because he has whiskers and a beard and is much more hairy. This is probably why he is generally more intelligent as well.' I heard him say more than once that Delilah, in cutting Samson's hair ('and she must have cut other things as well,' he would comment), had deprived him not only of his strength but also of his reason. Tesio did not have much hair and I think he felt that he needed a whole day's beard to have all the necessary intelligence to make a good purchase.

He was incapable of shaving himself and, whether he was in Rome, Milan or Pisa, he would go to a barber each morning after working his horses. At Newmarket the situation was more complicated. During the sales he had no timetable, the lots which interested him might come up at any time of the day. The barber insisted on making appointments—which Tesio never kept. Mr. Clayton, who was our host each year and who was well acquainted with Tesio's whims, thought he had solved the problem by arranging for the barber to call each morning at eight o'clock. The sales did not begin until nine so there could surely be no objection. On the second day the barber did not appear. Tesio had told him not to call again.

These fantastic notions were not always purely superstitious. Many had a scientific (or pseudo-scientific) basis but they had to have sufficient magical content as well.

There was the pendulum, sensitive to radiation. Tesio consulted it constantly. I suspect that he used it less to make decisions than to confirm decisions already taken. Since he never told anyone when he had made a decision, or what the decision was—and since no one else understood the turning or swaying of the pendulum—the answer it gave was never open to discussion.

Once, at Newmarket, he decided to buy a mare called Windsor Park. The catalogue stated that she was in foal but since the printing of the catalogue she had been found to be barren. We went to see the mare—and out came the pendulum. To the amazement of those present, Tesio began to explore her with the device: over her back and sides and under her tail. The answer was clearly satisfactory (to Tesio): 'She's pregnant!' The next day the mare was ours—barren! In time the purchase proved fruitful for Dormello-Olgiata and Windsor Park's descendants included many winners such as the excellent Viani.

The pendulum was superseded by sealing-wax. Sealing-wax rubbed on wool acts as a magnet to small pieces of paper. Tesio decided to put such a force to good use and for a while kept a piece of sealing-wax in his pocket reasoning that the contact with wool would keep it permanently active. On reflection, however, he felt that, if this force existed, it would exercise a particular influence over those parts of his anatomy which were in the immediate vicinity of the pocket—interesting possibilities but not useful ones in connection with his horses for which his cerebral faculties were the prime consideration. The sealing-wax was moved to the inside of his hat. There it remained attached by sticking-plaster until it, in turn, was replaced by a magnet, the attractive force of which was much more powerful than that of the sealing-wax.

The results of the changeover were apparently negligible. Then someone remarked that the effect was being cancelled by the little piece of metal which held the two sections of the magnet together—remove that and the circuit would be opened permitting the force to pass through Tesio's brain. He 'opened the circuit' instantly and, since the magnet was used in his latter years, it could be said that Ribot was the result!

If many of the claims he made lacked any real foundations and were almost always connected with his numerous superstitions, his lively intelligence did conceive many original ideas regarding the future. These seemed eccentric at the time but, in many cases, proved to be prophetic. For example, he used to say that if a way could be found to liberate the force which holds together the atoms of a diamond, the power unleashed would amount to millions of kilowatts. He believed that the hardness of the diamond was due to the force which held its atoms together. In this particular instance he was mistaken; although he had correctly imagined that atomic energy could be unleashed—and this many years before Nagasaki and Hiroshima.

And, if before a race Tesio went in for all sorts of hocus-pocus, after a victory he would stand, his two feet planted firmly on the ground, and reply to anyone who congratulated him with a characteristics phrase: 'Enough! Now let's get on.'

The eccentricities, superstitions and outbursts of rage which created the myth of Tesio, masked his deeper qualities of courage, energy, devotion to work, and endless perseverance, qualities that made the real man I recognised and came to know so well.

CHAPTER 7

Selling horses

WHEN IT CAME to selling his horses, Tesio knew no
hesitation. His answer was 'Yes' or 'No'. Only in
exceptional cases would he say that he must consult me
before making a decision, and this was a manoeuvre of
which I was always forewarned. If asked to name a price
he would name one; if an offer was made, he would accept
it. It was a good sales technique. On the one hand it suited
his idiosyncratic dislike for deliberation and, on the other,
it fell in with a well-known commercial principle—a
buyer who is not subject to bargaining will always pay
more than a harassed customer who feels under pressure.

Tesio sold both Donatello and Nearco without a
moment's hesitation.

Donatello was requested by telegram the day after the
Grand Prix de Paris, 1937, when he was runner-up. Tesio
immediately handed the sale over to me giving me the
broadest possible mandate. 'Get them to make an offer and
sell him.' It would never have entered Tesio's head to offer
the horse to an Italian breeder or to consult the Italian
Jockey Club first. To whom should he offer the horse
first? To a small-scale breeder who could not pay? To one
of the large-scale owner breeders who were in direct
competition with him? Consult the Jockey Club which
mistrusted and despised him? Never!

Tesio's telegram was from Mr. Edward Esmond who

had returned to England immediately after Donatello's race. Esmond was a guest of Mrs. Clayton at Newmarket and, as she was an intimate friend of Donna Lydia, the latter was able to ask if the negotiations for the sale of Donatello might take place at Mrs. Clayton's house, 'The Severals'. Mrs. Clayton agreed saying she was glad to help.

During race-weeks and during the sales, the most famous names in the English and French racing world would gather at this large and splendid house. For me they were acquaintances, not friends. Mrs. Clayton had met the Tesios at the December Sales some years before and continued to offer them hospitality each year during the sales. The shrewd and original little Italian, already well-known in England because of the amazing number of times he had won the Italian Derby (either he was a wizard or the Italian races were a joke), and his plain, tall, and distinguished wife, with her ducal airs and knowledge of human and equine pedigrees, 'did well' in Mrs. Clayton's drawing-room, where the conversation ran on horses from morning till night.

It might have been thought that Tesio, who spent nearly 365 days a year amongst racehorses, would have been happy to listen to the instructive conversation of the world's greatest experts on thoroughbreds. Not at all. After a couple of days he could stomach it no longer. By the end of the week he could think of nothing but escape. If he delayed his departure it was only because an interesting horse might go for a song on the last day when money was running short.

The monotony of the conversation ...! How one horse had won and another had lost ... how the narrator had bet, won, or lost. Tesio's increasing nausea came from the fact that he could learn nothing from all this. 'Pay no attention to what they say,' he would warn me, 'they judge horses only by how much they have won or lost on them.'

During one of Tesio's visits to Newmarket a pleasant young man came to stay at Mrs. Clayton's. Unlike the rest he was cultured, versatile, and good company. He had married a girl from a family of racing enthusiasts, though he himself knew nothing at all about horses or racing. Tesio wondered how such a lamb had fallen into that lions' den. The following year the whole family were Mrs. Clayton's guests—except for that young man. They had forced him to seek a divorce! 'How could the poor girl live with a man who had no interest in horses?'

Such was the set-up into which I was thrown in the role of leading actor. I left for Newmarket travelling by air to get there faster ('Esmond mustn't change his mind!'). I hate flying, and in 1937 it was even more detestable than it is today. Aeroplanes were not pressurised and whilst crossing the Alps we had to breathe oxygen from rubber tubes which insufflated the necessary gas into each passenger. There were paper mouth pieces and the company assured the passengers that these were changed for every flight. The journey seemed endless. The 'plane, which was Dutch, stopped at Frankfurt and went on to Amsterdam where passengers were transferred to an English 'plane. It was night when we flew from Amsterdam to Croydon (the flight, including stops and transfers, lasted between seven and eight hours) so I spent the night in London, took a train to Newmarket the following morning, and finally arrived at 'The Severals' some twenty-four hours after my departure from Milan.

My arrival in the drawing-room was greeted by a friendly: 'Ah, voici notre marquis!' from my hostess. I froze under the stares of the assembled guests. Mrs. Clayton, then between sixty and seventy years, retained the appearance of a beautiful and elegant English woman. In fact she was French and her wit and brilliant conversation were typically so.

Introductions followed. These were embarrassing. The English do not shake hands and the foreigner does not know what to do with his hand or where to put it. It was doubly embarrassing for me as I was introduced, as usual, as 'Tesio's partner'. For twenty-two years I was never considered in any other light in England. When I finally regained my own identity I became 'Ribot's owner'. Only after Ribot's death was I called Incisa.

My hostess asked me amiably whether I needed anything before starting negotiations with Mr. Esmond (whom I did not know and was trying to identify among those present). I said, rashly, that I would like to telephone to my wife at Olgiata. (At that time one still let people know that one had arrived safely, particularly after such a journey.) I should have expected Mrs. Clayton's immediate reply: 'To your wife? Already? Why such a hurry? Have you a bad conscience? Tell me, what were you up to in London last night?' My embarrassment must have been obvious because immediately her irony vanished and she said kindly: 'Now I'll give you a room to yourselves where you will be able to speak, discuss, and quarrel without being disturbed.'

At that moment an old man, with very white hair and whiskers and an olive complexion, rose from an armchair and came over to meet me. This, evidently, was Mr. Esmond and we were now able to shake hands before being shown into an attractive little room decorated in French eighteenth-century style. In that incongruous Pompadour setting, Esmond and I talked, discussed—but did not quarrel. He wanted to buy at all costs; I had been instructed to sell whatever happened.

The first stage of our negotiations consisted of futile attempts to discover our respective limits. We circled the subject, rather like dogs sniffing each other and raising their legs ritually a great many times. Eventually matters became a little more explicit. The first figures were mentioned, one still far from the other—a sort of karate in which lethal blows are threatened but not struck— otherwise the fun would be over. My £55,000 set against his £40,000 eventually became *our* £47,500.

Now it was tea-time and we found all the others in the dining room, just back from the races. Esmond and I had agreed not to disclose the eventual agreed price and, at tea, no one asked us. Half an hour later all Newmarket knew! I called Tesio and he was delighted. I think that if I had told him that I had accepted £20,000 he would have been just as satisfied. Donatello belonged to the past; he wanted to get on with the future.

The following year Nearco won the Grand Prix de Paris and the succession of events was the same: an immediate offer from England and Tesio's immediate consent. I was again put in charge of the negotiations and again told to 'sell him'. This time the journey was more comfortable—Flêche d'Or this side of the Channel, Golden Arrow the other; a room at Claridge's; a Daimler from London to Newmarket—Donatello had been a runner-up whilst Nearco was a winner, so I could be more lavish.

The negotiations proved simpler than those of the previous year. The British Bloodstock Agency—the B.B.A. of which Tesio had been a friend and client for a long time—had been instructed to act by Mr. Martin Benson, an important bookmaker. The director of the Agency at that time, Mr. Ernest Coussell, was in charge of the affair; a small, fair, plump man, aged somewhere between forty and fifty, with short-sighted eyes behind gold-framed spectacles. He looked like a dentist or a chemist, but soon showed that he knew the exact commercial value of every kind of horse. £60,000 was offered for Nearco. I accepted.

It was unthinkable that these negotiations should take place at Mrs. Clayton's house. Mr. Esmond was one thing, Coussell quite another. The problem for the Continental is to discover the basis on which such discrimination is made. No one will ever explain it. Donna Lydia had invented her own discriminations or had learned them from someone. But the English imbibe them with their mothers' milk, if they are not born with them.

Mr. Benson had decreed that we were to bring a reply to him at tea-time and, when we arrived, we found him drinking his tea, which was as black as coffee, from an enormous cup which must have held a pint or more. Mr. Esmond had negotiated for Donatello in terms which were both amiable and diplomatic. Mr. Benson did not negotiate, he bluntly asked whether I had accepted his offer. When I replied in the affirmative he just nodded his head as much as to say: 'I should think so. ...!'

There was nothing more to say. Mr. Coussell and I drank our tea in silence. It was very black but the size of the cups was normal.

Once again Tesio was delighted with the outcome. Probably I had been sent by Tesio to conclude these sales because of his reluctance to be away from the stables during the racing season. He confined his own travels to the winter months and the few weeks when the San Siro race-track was closed during the heat of the Italian summer.

On our annual pilgrimage to the December Sales, the

Tesios and I travelled separately, as the Tesios like to
spend a few days in Paris both on the way to Newmarket
and on the return journey. But the first year that I
returned to Newmarket after the war, I travelled for the
first (and last!) time with Tesio. I had persuaded him to
let me organise the trip from Switzerland as I happen to
be there at the time. Reluctantly he agreed. Would that I
had never thought of it! The journey must have been
arranged through a travel agency. Neither I nor, even less,
Tesio, could have struggled through the maze of post-war
timetables.

We left Lausanne for Berne in a *wagon ordinaire*
packed to bursting point with passengers (rather
ordinaire), and had to travel in the corridor, I seated on
my suit-case and Tesio on the ticket-collector's seat. It was
snowing and bitterly cold. Our improvised seating
arrangements were ventilated by the door of the W.C. and
the door leading to the next carriage; doors which opened
and shut with monotonous regularity, wafting gusts of
polar air with more than a hint of disinfectant. The
change at Berne brought the welcome lukewarm
atmosphere of a *wagon-lit* and a decided improvement in
our situation but, by the time we had reached Paris the
following morning, Tesio had had enough of trains and
declared that we would take the next 'plane to London.

We made our way to the Scribe, the hotel where Tesio
had always stayed before the war. It was very squalid.
Not only the décor but the staff too were showing traces of
the four years of occupation to which they had been
subjected. A surly hall porter informed us that no seats
were available on London flights until the following
morning: 'Well then, we will leave tomorrow morning!'
(The train on which we were booked was due to leave
almost at once and we could have been in London that

same evening, but that was out of the question. Tesio had
had enough of trains.)

We had to rise at four thirty the following morning to
be at the Gare d'Orsay air terminal on time. In the bleak
and barren hall of the terminal, seated on wooden
benches, we waited for four hours. There was fog at
Northolt. Then we were taken to Le Bourget to continue
our wait for a further two hours. Throughout Tesio
remained seated, staring fixedly ahead of him, his lower
lip jutting out aggressively. This discouraged any attempt
at conversation.

Due to our late arrival in London, a further stop-over
was called for—this time at the Berkeley Hotel. Here we
were shown to a luxurious suite with a hall, sitting-room,
bathroom and one, only one, twin-bedded room. Our
protests were to no avail. We were twenty-four hours later
than expected and this was the only accommodation
available. We were both exhausted so, without further
ado, we made ready for bed whilst pretending to ignore
each other.

It was during that night that I discovered why, for as
long as man could remember (or rather, as long as
chambermaid could remember) Donna Lydia had decline
to share, not only her husband's bed, but his room as well.

I drifted to sleep only to be woken shortly afterwards
by the eccentric use Tesio made of the night hours. He
turned the light on. Half an hour later he turned it off
again—then on again. He got up and, through half-closed
eyes I saw that he was wearing only a very brief pyjama
top. He had very white legs, a book in his hand, and
spectacles on his nose. He plumped his pillows, shook the
blankets, went back to bed—and then started all over
again.

In the middle of the night a new activity commenced. I

heard creaking, grating, rustling and rummaging. Unable to make it out I had to have a look. Tesio, in his scanty clothing, was transporting bed and bedding from the bedroom to the sitting-room. I was touched to see how, at his age, he was trying to make this complicated manoeuvre as silently as possible so as not to disturb me. I was tempted to jump out of bed to help but knew that he would have been mortified had he realised I was awake and watching.

It was a great relief when, the following day, we finally found ourselves in the cordial warmth of the Clayton household. Our delightful hosts always paid Tesio the courtesy of inviting his friends or people of interest to meet him at dinner. Such dinners were excellent, the cooking was entirely French and the exquisite wines were selected with care and presented with the respect they deserved.

I do not know why, but the guests of the Claytons were predominantly six foot-three or taller and to be examined from above by these towers with their impassive expressions—such as the English wear when they wish to be polite without being familiar or, heaven forbid, cordial—can be embarrassing and intimidating for anyone under five foot-eight. Tesio, however, five foot-five, was undeterred and totally uninhibited and, after a glass or two of wine, would give vent to his considerable talents as a raconteur. His incredible tales may not have been entirely truthful but they never failed to amuse and interest his fellow guests. He would happily flout convention, invariably failing to pass the port to his neighbour until discreetly prompted to do so by his host—and then he usually passed it in the wrong direction, which would have been an unpardonable crime in an Englishman. He spoke his terrible English in a very loud voice, inventing words as he went along, and yet everyone listened to him.

His bastardised language did not bother them at all. They appreciated his phenomenal success with horses and enjoyed his eccentric conversation and bizarre theories. They did not say, as did the Milanese, '*L'e matt!*' (he's crazy); he was Italian which, for them, may well have meant much the same thing.

Despite some bewilderment, Tesio was far better appreciated, and his work more fairly evaluated in England than it was in Italy. At Newmarket he was respected and Tesio felt this.

CHAPTER 8

The business man

INDUBITABLY TESIO WAS intelligent but he was not
a good businessman. *I* am not a good businessman so it
would have been better for both of us if we had stayed
away from those who were. With a little more caution and
circumspection we could have been more successful but we
did not know how to make the most of the opportunities
which presented themselves.

On one occasion, before the Second World War, Tesio
advised me to buy a piece of land known as Maura which
lies between his yard at San Siro (Milan) and the Trenno
Company's training grounds some half a mile away, in
order to set up new training grounds. These would have
greatly reduced the wear and tear of the Trenno grounds.
I was about to sign the contract when a representative of
the Trenno Company informed me that it would 'not be
correct for an associate of Tesio's to conduct such a
business establishment'. I was told that it would be 'much
appreciated if a company were to be formed to fulfil this
function, to the advantage of all the stables, under the
directorship of Marchese Incisa'.

I have yet to understand why a job which was
considered unworthy of Tesio's associate should become
respectable simply by that person acting in the guise of
Company President! As it worked out I became a minority
shareholder with the sweetening of the 'Presidency of the

Administrative Council', and the majority shareholdings were divided between Trenno, as a company, and representatives of Trenno as individuals. Rent for the land was paid by Trenno.

Then came war—separation of northern and southern Italy—aftermath of war—inflation—devaluation. A vote was called by the President for the rent to be raised to the level of devaluation with the predictable result that the rent had to be that of 1939! A proposal was put forward to amalgamate Maura and Trenno; eleven shares from Maura to one from Trenno—approved! The *President* lost his seat and face!

The second business venture upon which, on the advice of Tesio, I embarked concerned a racing yard in Rome. When Tesio was nominated Senator he was required to attend at least some of the meetings of the Upper Chamber and this meant that, from time to time, he had to leave his horses. To Tesio this was an impossible situation. He decided that it would be best for the horses to winter in Rome which necessitated the building of a yard with forty to fifty boxes. He reasoned that, as the Milanese yard belonged to him, it was only fair that the yard in Rome should belong to me and be built at my expense. (I cannot remember the actual price but, bearing in mind the layout, as planned by Tesio, it must have been a colossal sum.)

The yard was completed in 1941 and, due to the war, was empty from 1943 onwards. The horses stayed in Milan! In 1944 it was taken over by evacuees and became the headquarters of Rome's black market. Eventually I requested an eviction order but after an attempt to carry out the order, during which the police were put to flight, I was advised to let the matter drop.

With considerable difficulty I eventually managed to

sell the yard, still occupied, for a paltry sum. The property had been mine—and the loss was exclusively mine!

At the beginning of the war, it must have been late in 1939 or the beginning of 1940, suddenly and unexpectedly the Aga Khan offered *all* his horses, English and Irish, to Tesio. He gave no indication of price saying only that he would come to Milan for discussions if his offer was not refused outright. A meeting was arranged.

Tesio seemed surprisingly sceptical regarding a successful outcome. The meeting took place at the Hotel Principe di Savoia. Tesio felt, as I did, that the Italian state of 'non-belligerence' was very precarious but the Aga Khan was adamant that Mussolini was far too intelligent to lead Italy into a blatantly suicidal undertaking. The Aga seemed anxious to bring the deal to a rapid conclusion; evidently he was convinced that an invasion of England was imminent and that Ireland would then no longer be a safe refuge.

To our amazement we were asked a price which was somewhere between a fifth and a tenth of any valuation we might have put on this unequalled group of some two hundred horses among which was included not only Mumtaz Begum (who was carrying Nasrullah at the time), but the stallions Blenheim, Bahram and Mahmoud.

But, attractive though the prospect undoubtedly was, the Aga Khan made three absolute and unbreakable conditions: the entire payment was to be made immediately and in dollars; simultaneously we would have to take possession of all the horses (not the lands or stables, which would remain his property), and, at the same time, we would have become responsible for all expenses, including the staff in both England and Ireland. These conditions posed insuperable problems. How, and at what price, could the dollars be obtained! How could all the horses be transported to Italy with the wartime shortage of transport and the dangers facing shipping? And where could we put them? How could the staff be employed and paid? They would certainly not have been accepted in Italy at that time.

We explained to the Aga that, attracted as we were by his offer, we were not in a position to handle it on our own and would need Government assistance. The Aga Khan, being accustomed to the British Government's attitude to bloodstock, saw no problem in this. Convinced that the Italian authorities would recognise such a remarkable opportunity, he returned to 'Free' France to await the outcome. Tesio and I went to Rome and a meeting with the Minister of Agriculture. To our astonishment the advisors to the Minister found the price, which we had judged ridiculously small, exorbitant!

We went to see 'influential friends' (we considered them 'friends'—they considered themselves 'influential'), but to no avail. After a few hectic days of meetings, appointments, and discussions, we were forced to resign ourselves to the failure of the operation. An opportunity which could have altered the quality of Italian racing was lost.

I took the defeat very much to heart but Tesio did not share my disappointment. In retrospect I think that, had 'operation Aga Khan' been possible and, had it taken place entirely to *his* advantage or to that of Dormello-Olgiata, it would have suited him well but, since Government aid was indispensable to the project, it would necessarily have worked to the advantage of Italian racing as a whole—and Tesio was not at all inclined to put himself out to the advantage of his competitors and compatriots. It was already much if he did not do anything against their interests but, to actually go out of his way to help them, well—no! After all, if the great Aga Khan had produced Blenheim, Bahram and Mahmoud he, little Tesio, had produced Cavaliere d'Arpino, Donatello and Nearco and, without knowing it, he had already laid the foundations for Ribot. (Barbara Burrini had been at Dormello for three years.)

All that mattered to Tesio was to win stakes, any prize, even the smallest. It was not greed for money itself but the necessity to have as much of it at his disposal as possible in order to be able to buy better mares, use better stallions and so to create better racehorses—horses such as had never been seen before.

In 1932 we, the Incisas, had 'set up' his stable again. Immediately after the war even greater funds were offered to him when Avvocato Agnelli let it be known that he was willing to take shares in Dormello-Olgiata. Tesio thought of accepting the offer and asked me. I refused. Possibly I was selfish in refusing to give up a part of my share and perhaps I was also short-sighted. Maybe, had we accepted the offer, the stable would now be able to compete more successfully with the present importers of high-class racehorses.

Donna Lydia with the Count of Turin (circa 1905)

Tesio with Camici and Chauffeur

In his later years

CHAPTER 9

Tesio's principles of mating

ONE DAY AT Dormello, Tesio suddenly said to me: 'Come with me and I will show you how to do the matings.'

It was so unlike Tesio to take the trouble to teach anyone anything (I imagine that my 'lesson' must have been instigated by Donna Lydia) that I ought to remember the day, month and year of such a memorable event. In fact, I only know that it was summertime when the gates of the ˙race-track of Milan were closed for the summer break. (During these summer weeks Tesio never missed his siestas. After lunch he would spend a couple of hours or so on his bed or resting in an armchair, alternately dozing and reading.)

I seated myself next to him, all eyes and ears, trying to make the most of such an unprecedented opportunity and avoided asking too many questions which I knew would only irritate him.

'Here, look at this,' he said, thumbing his way through the split-pedigree book which accompanied him everywhere. The book, which had been carefully compiled by Donna Lydia, had an index which Tesio systematically ignored (or did he feel that turning pages at random might lead to a better combination?). Over the years the well-thumbed edges had become worn and grubby. A suitable mare was found and the search for the stallion began.

'Now, here there is St. Simon in the second generation of the stallion and down here he appears in the third generation in the mare: third and fourth go well in the offspring. Then he is by Bayardo and she by Sundridge. I would have preferred it the other way up but it's a "nick" which never fails—splendid!'

'And look at this other mare. I have always sent her to a Phalaris line horse because he is right for her' (no reason given), 'but she has never produced anything any good; now I'll try Son-in-Law and we will see what happens. Sometimes if you make what would seem an obvious mistake' (no explanation why it was a 'mistake') 'you get it right. It's a complete outcross. I try a few every year—sometimes it works, sometimes it doesn't. This year I will give this one a try.'

Whilst speaking he indicated the names on the pages with the back of his hand in a characteristic gesture. When referring to the less well-known names, he stroked the pages as though brushing crumbs from a tablecloth; 'This doesn't count: it's worth *nothing.*' My task was to listen and learn but it seemed courteous to show an interest by making an occasional remark or a query or, modestly, proposing an alternative idea. 'No, no it won't work—you must do it my way,' and it was pointless to ask why. Perhaps there *was* no reason why, so Tesio would change the subject of conversation.

Occasionally he would explain a preference. The explanation was a long and detailed disquisition taking in the biological and physiological aspects, and often astrological ones as well. The inevitable conclusion was that, as he had studied the matter from every angle, his way was the only way which could possibly work.

For fifty years results proved that, on the whole, his decisions were right and his methods sound, if methods there were—but this we shall never know. Perhaps it was a secret no one shared, not even Donna Lydia who, for half a century, recorded the names, pedigrees and comments which he dictated to her without discussion or objection to the matings he ordained. Tesio's word on the matter was gospel. Or perhaps there was no method as such but an intuition which he would not have been able to analyse or define. However that may be, I still wonder why in the world, on that particular day, he had decided to teach me 'how to do the matings'.

We used to play a game at Dormello. Tesio, Donna Lydia, my wife and I would each select our choice from the current crop of yearlings. The names would be put in a sealed envelope to be opened a couple of years later. When this happened Tesio's intuition was apparent, although it would have been impossible to define the basis on which he had made his choice, for it was certainly not based on conformation. Eventually I became convinced that Tesio had the knack to see into a horse's 'morale'.

I well recollect an occasion in 1948 when Colonel Scrope, stud manager to Lord Derby, asked Tesio to give an opinion on Borealis, perhaps as a possible successor to Hyperion. Hyperion was then eighteen years old, Borealis was seven. An energetic and athletic individual, he was by Brumeux out of Hyperion's daughter Aurora, who was also the dam of Alycidon the best horse in England that year. Everyone presumed to see in Borealis a striking resemblance to his maternal grandsire. Tesio just glanced at Borealis and came out of the box mumbling with scorn. He then asked if he could see Hyperion again, who was in a box nearby. There he stood for several minutes as though contemplating a masterpiece.

Hyperion had become rather dipped in his back with age, his rump was curiously horizontal and he had the somewhat vacant expression of an old horse—yet Tesio looked at him ecstatically. Sixteen years before I had seen him gaze at that same horse, then a two-year-old, barely bigger than a pony, and predict that his would become one of the great names in Turf history. The prediction, as everyone knows, came true.

As for Borealis, who speaks of him now?

The only way to learn from Tesio was to copy the method by which apprentices, during the Middle Ages, learnt the skills of humble craftsmen and great artists by keeping watch over a considerable period, endeavouring gradually to discover how the work should be done. But, whereas every painter, sculptor or craftsman had a particular way of working, a style which was a starting point giving direction to the apprentice, Tesio had no particular style or method, as he would continually and unexpectedly alter his pattern according to circumstance. Thus he had no disciples; he was, and remains, inimitable.

But, if his 'flair' cannot be acquired, it is possible by analysing his work as a breeder, to discover certain principles to which he always adhered:

(a) Never remain attached to your own female lines but revive the stud constantly with new families. (Tesio's means were modest but he never failed to purchase two or three mares or fillies annually. During his lifetime this process caused the gradual but constant replacement of most of the female lines which he used.)

(b) Avoid standing your own stallion. If the horse is successful the temptation is to sell all the nominations; if he is not then the temptation is to use him on your own mares since the nominations cost nothing. (Tesio successfully avoided this situation until the war when the transport of mares to other studs became virtually impossible. For the same reasons Tesio would not take shares in syndicated stallions.)

(c) Proven sires should always be preferred, even old and expensive ones, to the young, unproven horse—even though the latter may have been highly successful on the racecourse.

(d) Send your best mares to the best stallions. One high-class horse in a year is plenty and is preferable to a good average.

(e) Include a few close inbreedings, a few complete outcrosses, one or two proven blood affinities, (or 'nicks'), and one or two 'crosses' which it is felt could become 'nicks', in the annual mating list. (Tesio always observed this practice.)

(f) Attach tremendous importance to the annual inspection of all stallions to be used in the coming season. This will give a fresh and accurate picture of the conformation of each stallion—for the condition of a stallion can affect the outcome of the covering and the quality of the offspring. (Each winter Tesio would make long and exhausting journeys travelling to one stud after another throughout England and northern France to examine the stallions of his choice.)

(g) The *thoroughbred* exists because its selection has depended, not on experts, technicians, or zoologists, but on a piece of wood: the winning post of the Epsom Derby. If you base your criteria on anything else, you will get something else, not the thoroughbred. (This was one of Tesio's most basic convictions, nowadays regarded by many as little more than an antiquated prejudice. He maintained that: 'for almost two cen-

turies the conditions of the Derby have remained
unchanged and its validity unquestioned; it is the
Epsom Derby which has made the thoroughbred what
it is today'.)

A natural consequence of this 'Epsom' conviction, was
Tesio's insistence that a pedigree should contain as much
classic blood as possible. Whilst he would tolerate certain
pure sprint lines, provided they were not closer than the
fourth generation, he regarded what he termed 'classic
failures', horses with classic pedigrees but which turned
out to be milers or short distance horses, as 'clean speed'.

But, if he was diffident regarding sprinters, the quality
in a horse which most excited him was acceleration. He
believed that 'the best horse is the one which can win from
any point in a race—at five furlongs, a mile, or in the last
hundred yards.' He recognised that Nearco had this
quality to an extent unmatched by any other horse he had
trained.

It is strange that Tesio was acutely aware of this and
yet he never had a mare covered by Nearco. He never gave
a reason for this and I never asked him. I knew full well
that he would have answered with the first thing which
came into his head and that it would certainly not have
been the truth! It could have been the cost. When we first
returned to England after the war, nominations to Nearco
were already making £1,000 whereas Hyperion, already
established as a *chef de race*, did not then exceed £400.
Perhaps it was one of his whims; he had sold the horse
and was finished with him and, like certain children who
know they are in the wrong, he would not admit it. It is
possible that Tesio, despite Nearco's instant success as a
sire of winners, did not believe that this success would be
perpetuated through future generations or that Nearco's

singular powers of acceleration would be transmitted so forcefully to his direct descendants in the third and fourth generations—to produce Nijinsky, Sir Ivor, and Mill Reef.

Earlier in this chapter I referred to 'nicks', the affinity between unrelated lines of blood which can contribute to the success of certain matings. Tesio attached great importance to these affinities.

At one time the 'nick' between Bayardo and Sundridge was very successful, then a little later it was Hurry On and Bachelor's Double. On the subject of 'nicks' it was amusing to hear Tesio's account of the circumstances leading up to and following his purchase of a mare named Bella Minna from Lord Woolavington. Lord Woolavington owned Hurry On and had bought Bella Minna, a daughter of Bachelor's Double, to send to him. It seemed a perfect match but Bella Minna's offspring from this classic mating, confidently repeated year after year, were utter failures. Disheartened, Lord Woolavington decided to sell the mare and, rather than waste a further nomination to Hurry On, had her covered by the lesser stallion, Singapore.

Seeing her in the sale catalogue, Tesio decided that, as she had been a useful racemare but had failed when put to a stallion seemingly 'made to measure' for her, the more 'unsuitable' horse to which she was now in foal, just might mean that she would do better. Certainly the result could not be worse—and Tesio expected her price to reflect her poor performance at stud. It did—and he purchased her; the result was the successful Bistolfi, followed a few years later by Bellini, a forebear of Ribot.

Bella Minna had produced an unusual example of a spectacular failure of a seemingly certain 'nick'. Another affinity was that between Blandford and Clarissimus.

In December, 1933, Baron Robert de Nexon, Mr.

Wertheimer's stud manager and a guest, as were the Tesios and I, of the Claytons at Newmarket, told us with enthusiasm of an exceptional two-year-old colt he had seen in France. The colt was by Blandford, out of Vitamine by Clarissimus, and was bred by Baron Edouard de Rothschild—Brantôme. Three years later we had a two-year-old, also exceptional, by Blenheim, (a son of Blandford), out of Delleana by Clarissimus—Donatello. Delleana was, therefore, covered by Blenheim in the spring of 1933 before anything was known of Brantôme and Tesio considered with pride that it was he who had discovered this affinity.

Whilst we are on the subject of Tesio's successful breeding activities, I must take the opportunity to contradict the widely held belief that Tesio *forgot* to enter Ribot for the Italian Derby. Ribot was not entered for the race because Tesio did not wish to enter him. There is no need to make excuses for Tesio and, were he still alive, he would not want them. Tesio *did not forget* and did not make a mistake.

Tesio did not like Ribot's dam, Romanella who, after winning her early two-year-old races with ease, failed in the big Premio Chiusura and, worse still, began suffering from ringbones. Ribot's sire, Tenerani, had had an honourable career on the Italian and international racecourses and had been the first Dormello horse to win in England. He had proved himself to be a horse of Tesio's stamp; he was tough, an inexhaustible stayer—able to withstand the most testing gallops, and he remained sound throughout his career. But, as a stallion, Tesio disliked him more and more. It may have been due either to the fact that Tenerani was a rig—or because he used to climb the walls of his box. (This trick became so bad that we had to put a net halfway up the box to restrain him.) Further, he had to have a sheep as a companion. Perhaps it was just that he was an unattractive horse with a troublesome character which did not change. The final proof of Tesio's lack of interest in Tenerani came when I told him that we had received an offer of £20,000 for him, from England. 'Throw him at them!' was the instant reply.

Tesio disliked Romanella and despised Tenerani. Ribot was born of these two and *that* is why he was not entered for the Derby.

Ribot was rather small both as a foal and as a yearling. He was considered plain and yet, if you analysed him, it was impossible to fault his conformation. His coat was whole, rather dull bay, without a trace of white to add 'character'. It was precisely physical character which Ribot lacked. He was not an attractive horse and he disliked human company. Later, when Tesio was already very ill and Ribot started working as a two-year-old, I asked our jockey, Camici, whether he preferred Ribot or the promising filly Theodorica. He replied that Theodorica's action was more beautiful but that to ride Ribot was 'like sitting in an armchair'. Camici always tended to understate but, if that was the best he could say of Ribot, there seemed no reason for Tesio to beat his breast for having left him out of the Derby. In fact, in his first two races as a two-year-old, it was Ribot himself who seemed to be 'sitting in an armchair' and, on both occasions, only narrowly avoided defeat. It was only after these two races that Ribot finally understood what was required of him.

CHAPTER 10

Breeding

WHILST TESIO WAS still alive an article appeared in a newspaper which greatly praised him as a 'breeder' of horses. Donna Lydia took great exception to this and violently attacked the author as she held that everyone ought to recognise that Tesio's achievements as a 'trainer' were greater than his achievements as a 'breeder'.

The Dormello stud was internationally famous and it was known that Tesio had set it up, but relatively few people knew that Tesio trained the horses he raised. Why was Donna Lydia so emphatic on this occasion? The conviction could not have originated from Tesio's own statements, nor from the Italian racing fraternity or foreign sources. An opposite view was held. Perhaps, subconsciously, Donna Lydia thought of Dormello and the stud as her domain whereas no-one could dispute that the racing stable was entirely her husband's concern. His training methods were unique in Italy—as was the end to which they were the means—to produce a superhorse and then to exploit it.

He believed that careful breeding was the starting-point and was convinced that his ruthless training programme was essential to prove the excellence of the pedigree and to produce those hidden resources which only the severest of tests could yield. The superhorse must not break down otherwise it was unworthy of the name. Horses unable to stand up to his training methods were of no interest to Tesio.

Before a major race Tesio would often subject a contender to two trials over the full distance. Sometimes both trials would take place within a week of the race. Each time Tesio's attitude seemed to be 'make or break' (often 'break' is exactly what they did). By June, Tesio knew the value of each of his horses. He sold those which were worth little and sold them well for they were unexposed on the racecourse—although they had been thoroughly tried on the gallops early in the morning when only he knew the weights of each and the orders given to the work-riders.

No other owner would have used such extreme methods. The 'co-owner' did not have much say in the matter but shared the hope that one day there would be a superhorse in the stable.

Tesio was passionately interested in genetics and biology. He was well informed regarding De Vries' theory on mutations and had a theory of his own: the *law of the unstable maxima.* He realised that, without a relevant and revolutionary variation, all horses would conform to the original and none of them, however well-bred or trained, would rise far enough above the norm to pulverise an adversary on the racecourse. The horse Tesio was looking for must, by definition, be abnormal, a freak, an equine prodigy.

Perhaps, with this in mind, he would solemnly maintain that a long horse always has an advantage over a short one because 'in a race of 1,000 metres, a horse a kilometre long would win before starting!' This was precisely the sort of remark which drove the Italian racing élite into a frenzy of irritation. Tesio was undoubtedly intelligent so why did he come out with these remarks? Was it to make fools of them? Possibly ...

Then Naucide was foaled; a dark bay colt, (a colour much favoured by Tesio), by Bellini and out of Tesio's beloved Nogara, he had a large head, short neck, small straight shoulder-blades, was very short through his loins, had enormous quarters, and an exaggeratedly sloping rump. He was rather high on the leg but much higher at the back than at the withers.

Tesio was enchanted by him. The newborn foal had all the characteristics of a hare, except for the ears. ('Hares are very speedy, five times as speedy as horses if you take their respective dimensions into account!'). Perhaps the longed-for prodigy had finally arrived. The foal was certainly a freak. As he grew he did not, as so often happens, become more normal. To Tesio's immense satisfaction Naucide's horrible features became more accentuated. Logically, if his half-brother Nearco had been as good as he was in spite of lacking Naucide's undoubtedly distinctive features, the latter could not fail to be superior to him. Added to this he was inbred 2×3 to Havresac II who, in turn, was inbred 2×3 to St. Simon— whom Tesio held to be the best horse of all time.

Unfortunately, when it came to racing, Naucide was less than mediocre—which struck a great blow at the theory of the 'freak prodigy'. Four years later it seemed that Teniers might make up for Naucide's failure and that the theory of the 'freak prodigy' could be reconsidered.

Teniers was a pale chestnut, his mane and tail almost white: he was gigantic but as narrow as a knife blade and extremely ugly. Tesio considered him ugly until he saw his first canters. His action was astonishing. Never before had Tesio seen a comparable length of stride. The only expression to describe it is 'liquid'. Hardly anyone

remembers Teniers but I remember him well and I
remember Tesio's emotion as he watched him carefully to
discover whether 'the motor matched the coachwork'. Alas,
it did not; the 'motor' had no acceleration and, despite his
'liquid' action, he was all too easily liquidated by the most
humble adversaries.

Donatello and Nearco had been the products of
orthodox matings and, though they were of quite different
conformation, both were completely normal horses. The
idea that the superhorse would necessarily be a freak, the
result of a mutation so that he would be born unlike his
ancestors, developed late in Tesio's life when he had
become afflicted with that sense of urgency which is a
characteristic of the old; the desire to carry through and
complete, before it is too late, any project which has been
started. When sixty-five years old, Tesio had been full of
the exuberance and energy of youth; when he felt that his
life was nearing its end, he desperately wanted a sensational success.

1934 was the first year that the foals born at Dormello
were sent, as weanlings, to winter at Olgiata, my family
property near Rome. Nearco and Donatello were amongst
them. I had then been associated with Tesio for only two
years. Tesio realised that these sheep pastures, which had
never carried horses, would be an ideal complement to the
Dormello paddocks. (He said that, 'if it had not been for
the fences, hedges, and other impedimenta on the land
between Dormello and Olgiata, the horses could have
migrated in autumn and set out for Dormello in spring'.)
Donatello and Nearco fulfilled his expectations.

Oddly enough I have no recollection of Donatello's
presence at Olgiata, although I was living there at the
time. Even then he must have been considered special
being by Blenheim, winner of the English Derby, and out

of the great Delleana, but I remember very little of his two-year-old career. The victories that year—Bernina, Brueghel, Ettore Tito, Tofanella, Ugolino da Siena, Sorolla, Tempesta—there were so many winners in 1936—had probably made me blasé so that it seemed no more than normal that a good-looking, well-bred colt, trained by Tesio, should remain unbeaten.

The following year there was a crisis when Donatello, then at Pisa, went lame. Tesio, who claimed to have sound veterinary knowledge, was puzzled. Professor Galli, a famous veterinary expert who was at that time Director of the Veterinary Clinic at Pisa University, was consulted and pronounced that the lameness originated in the foot. The farrier was called to remove the shoe. Inevitably he disagreed with Professor Galli's diagnosis, (in the Professor's absence), and was reluctant to remove the shoe although, finally, he gave in. To the farrier's evident and understandable satisfaction, the lameness did not disappear when the shoe was removed and it was some days later that it vanished, without further treatment, to leave us all speculating uselessly on the causes of the infirmity.

In spite of his sudden recovery, Donatello did not run either at Pisa or in the Premio Parioli but went on to win with ease the Italian Derby, the Gran Premio d'Italia, and the Gran Premio di Milano. This last was regarded as a trial for the Grand Prix de Paris (which in those days still carried great prestige as it enabled the three-year-olds to tackle the best of the older horses for the first time).

Although the Milan race was regarded solely as a trial, it was not considered surprising that it was run only a week before the Grand Prix. Certainly this did not disturb Tesio; in his younger days horses had to be heroic to withstand training and probably the preparatory race was, from the horses' point of view, a milder alternative than the pitiless gallops which would otherwise have been inflicted.

In any case it would have been impossible to have galloped Donatello during that week. He could not leave for Paris on the Monday because we had to see how he was after the Milan race but, on the Tuesday, he had to set out on the gruelling journey travelling in an ordinary railway truck. The journey took two-and-a-half days so that, when he arrived on the Thursday evening, it was only possible to give him a short walk. On the Friday he had a canter, on the Saturday a 'pipe-opener', and on the Sunday he raced. Donatello had the constitution and the temperament to emerge unscathed by such treatment. He did not fret as most thoroughbreds do and seemed absolutely nerveless.

A big chestnut horse, he stood over a lot of ground and had good bone and a powerful frame. He gave the impression of being exceptionally robust and solid. He was said to be of the Bend Or type although, unlike that horse, he had very sloping quarters a characteristic which, Tesio always insisted, had only come into evidence after St. Simon—of whom Donatello had four lines in his pedigree. This was not accidental. Tesio was never afraid to include as much St. Simon blood in a pedigree as he could.

Donatello was a big-actioned horse and it may have been this which caused him to drift in his races. For this reason his bridle was always equipped with a prickly pad between the near side ring of the bit and his mouth—but this age-old expedient was not very effective in Donatello's case. Because of the horse's inability to corner, Tesio's orders to the jockey, Gubellini, (in the Grand Prix), were explicit: he was to remain on the rail with other horses on his outside so that he could not run wide. The result was that Donatello was shut in and, by the time Gubellini was able to extricate him, it was too late—he was unable to get up in time and finished second.

Gubellini, a very outspoken man, complained angrily to me after the race saying: 'Another time I'll pay no attention to his orders!' (The following year Gubellini rode Nearco, his own way, and won. But, of course, Nearco was a very different horse from Donatello, much easier to handle and perhaps the better of the two. It is also probable that, in Nearco's case, Tesio did not think it necessary to tell Gubellini how to ride him.)

Immediately after the Grand Prix we received an offer for Donatello proving that he could, and should, have won the race. Exactly the same situation had arisen eleven years before after Apelle had finished unplaced in the same race. Ridden to Tesio's orders, the horse had led throughout the race at an incredible pace only to be passed, almost on the post, by four inferior horses. An offer of £26,000 was made for him immediately after the race—an enormous sum at that time especially since the horse was not even placed. Clear enough evidence that the horse was not to blame for the defeat.

To give an account of Nearco it is necessary to begin at the mating which produced him. The search for a suitable stallion for Nogara had been particularly careful and laborious. She was one of Tesio's great favourites. As for all mares which were covered abroad, there were many details to be considered; the foaling date, the date on which the arduous train journey should be undertaken, the ability of the mare to withstand such a journey, the quality of the stud where she would live for six or seven months and the competence of the stud groom of that stud, the peculiarities of the stallion, and so forth. With all these considerations in mind, Tesio had selected Fairway.

The pedigree seemed perfect and Fairway's conformation seemed an ideal complement to Nogara. He was a big horse and rather long, whereas she was small and compact. He had won the St. Leger, whereas her maximum distance was a mile-and-a-quarter. Fairway belonged to Lord Derby and, until a short time before, his stud has been managed by Mr. Alston, a long standing friend and admirer of Tesio. Mr. Alston had died and his place had been taken by a certain Captain Paine, (whose military bearing and bristling red moustache made me wonder if he was *the* Captain Jack Paine). He did not have the slightest idea who Tesio was. Had Mr. Alston been alive Tesio would have been granted a nomination to Fairway with enthusiasm. Paine was another matter and he refused point blank. I remember today the impassive expression which accompanied this refusal.

Tesio was in despair. He was convinced that the mating was right, the pedigree perfect. Reluctantly he decided to send Nogara to Pharos, a full brother to Fairway but physically his opposite being a compact, muscular horse, much more typical of their sire, Phalaris who was, in truth, only a miler despite having been placed second to Papyrus in the Derby.

As so often happens when one is obliged to settle for the second-best, the result was perfect. The French stud where Pharos stood was excellent, the stud groom competent and trustworthy, the stallion covered successfully (and, in addition, the cost was considerably less than would have been the case with Fairway—in later years Pharos was to become much more sought after as a sire than his brother), and Nogara's foaling was entirely normal.

When Nogara returned from France, the foal she carried raised no great expectations in Tesio. He was convinced that stayers were declining and that there was already too much fast blood being put into the breed. He did not particularly want a sprinter, or at best, a miler. When Nogara foaled Tesio examined the newly born colt and grunted his approval. It was as he expected and had predicted, a little miler but well made for the job.

Nearco's character began to assert itself after weaning when he arrived to winter at Olgiata. He would never leave his companions alone in the paddock and, by way of a game, would deliberately shove them with his shoulder so that they staggered away from him. He was strong and stocky, what was known in the old Roman *campagna* as a 'winner'. Tesio was delighted when he saw him again. He liked the youngster's aggressiveness. 'I will make something of this one,' he declared and, from then on, he was constantly asking for news of him.

Nearco was incredibly tough. During his training he took whatever came his way, under whatever weight he was given, and could have been ridden by the proverbial 'sack of potatoes'. It was impossible to add anything to his capabilities by extra work or to subtract anything by reducing it because he did exactly what he wanted, in the way he wanted. Tesio no longer found it particularly amusing to train him. If he had any doubts and devised some new and more difficult trial, the horse made light of it. When he ran he won, it was a matter of indifference to him. Afterwards he would just eat and rest. He did not even bother to become difficult or bad tempered as horses so often do when they become aware of being special.

It was like a dream. There was never even the slightest hitch in his career, not even a touch of colic or a moment's lameness. Unbeaten in his two-year-old races, he went on at three to take the Premio Parioli, the Italian Derby, the

Gran Premio d'Italia, the Gran Premio di Milano and, finally, the Grand Prix de Paris.

I stood with Tesio on the stands at Longchamp for the Grand Prix 1938. He stood motionless and silent watching Nearco's every stride as though spurring him on with his eyes. As Nearco sailed effortlessly past the winning post, Tesio let go and, giving me a great thump on the back, he let out a cry of triumph. It was not an 'Oh!' of satisfaction but the full throated and terrible 'Aaah!' of Attila the Hun when, having raped, pillaged and plundered, he decapitated with one stroke of his scimitar the bishop who knelt begging him to spare the cathedral!

Tesio's great dream had come true and, thank God, he had lived to see it.

CHAPTER 11

Conversation—amusing and otherwise

TESIO HAD GREAT favourites amongst his horses and would lavish attention on them to the virtual exclusion of the other horses in the yard. Numbered in this select band were Guido Reni, Michelangelo, Apelle, Delleana, Cavaliere d'Arpino, Gerard, Nogara, Navarro, Tofanella, Donatello, and Trevisana. Strangely, Nearco was not amongst the favourties, although Tesio recognised his superb qualities; nor were Niccolo del'Arca or Tenerani despite the immense satisfaction they had given Tesio at home and abroad.

Amongst the favourties, Cavaliere d'Arpino reigned supreme. Even after his experiences with Donatello and Nearco, Tesio still believed Cavaliere d'Arpino to be the best horse he had ever trained. Had he lived to witness Ribot's triumphs I am quite sure that Tesio would have attributed the merit to that horse's great-grand sire, Cavaliere d'Arpino.

For Nogara Tesio had a tender admiration and I think that, for him, she represented the thoroughbred at its most perfect. Her conformation might well have been used as a model for an illustration in a veterinary manual and the lines of her limbs were perfection. I remember how Tesio would gaze at her when she was at exercise and his repeated: 'Look, look at the power she has behind, how well her hocks are let down. There is no deviation, no waste, it's all propulsive force.' But, above all, it was her effortless swinging gallop, seemingly activated by a steel spring, which completely entranced Tesio.

I have often wondered if Ribot's action would have excited Tesio in the same way. Unfortunately, by the time Ribot went into training, Tesio was too ill to continue the gruelling routine he had followed for half a century. He was frail and weak, felt the cold as he had never done before, and was almost blind. On his increasingly rare visits to the stables, Ugo Penco or Camici would describe the morning's gallops to him. It is improbable that he saw Ribot's first canters, impossible that he could have judged them, and unthinkable that he could have mentally compared Ribot's action with that of Nogara. Their action was similar save in one respect; Ribot had a peculiarity which was, I think, unique. He galloped like a dog, giving the impression of striking the ground with both hind feet simultaneously. I say 'giving the impression' because no animal, not even a dog, really gallops that way; it would cause loss of balance and one of Ribot's characteristics when galloping was his perfect balance. At whatever speed he moved, he remained completely unruffled, a perfect combination of balance and rhythm.

'Rhythm is everything,' Tesio would say. 'All nature has rhythm, where there is rhythm there is order, measure, harmony. Without rhythm there is chaos, ruin and catastrophe. Storms, hurricanes, earthquakes, these are the anti-rhythms of the cosmos—and the way some jockeys ride a finish is chaotic, ruinous and catastrophic!'

When giving orders to a jockey Tesio constantly repeated the same instruction: 'Give him time to find his legs; when you feel he has found them—go! And, when he has found his rhythm, then start to regulate the pace. Try to go a little more. If he responds, go with him and ask for a little more—*and a little more—and a little more.* Go a little more than the horse beside you or just behind you wants to go—then they won't be able to sprint off and beat you.'

It was this tactic of 'waiting in front' which Tesio used to win with horses such as Cavaliere d'Arpino, Donatello, and Nearco, which had no need for pacemakers. But, if he judged that a horse did need a companion to set the pace, he was adamant that they should race close together. It irritated him beyond measure to see a pacemaker detach himself from the field and go tearing off alone.

'What is the use of a pacemaker if he is ten, twelve, fifteen lengths ahead? Believe me, some of the people giving orders have no idea what they are doing. They think there is nothing to being a trainer, that all you have to do is watch the others and copy them! The owners are as bad, they copy each other when they buy horses, when they engage trainers, when they mate their mares. I copy no one. I have no method. Method is imitation—I *invent.* And, because the others have never seen what I do before, they say I am mad. But, if they try to imitate me, I have already invented something else, so they are still left behind. I have never imitated anyone, in breeding or in training. The world would be in a fine state by now if people had only imitated one another since time began. Nothing would have changed since Adam and Eve—and, in horse-racing, nothing since Eclipse. Horses would still be running in four heats of three miles at fifteen miles an hour!

'The most idiotic thing man can do is to imitate. The result is decadence! Look what happens in art when an original style becomes a fashion. Some painters even imitate their own work if it is successful: Boldini, Sargent, Whistler ... but that at least is *honest* imitation. But what would you think of someone who makes copies by painting photographs of his own pictures? Yet a printer showed me some photographs of paintings, printed on paper as thin as muslin, which the painter himself would have stuck onto canvas and painted over! He was very successful in America and there are two or three pages about him in an Italian *Enciclopedia*. Thief! Scoundrel! Rascal! To prostitute art, which is sacred. They put pickpockets and robbers in gaol—but they are gentlemen by comparison!'

This rambling discussion was typical of Tesio's lively and entertaining conversation. It was his way of airing and developing his own ideas. Many of these ideas concerned horses and racing and were original, to say the least.

'Everyone knows that the tension felt at the start of a severe athletic test partially inhibits breathing. Skiers, runners, and jumpers are trained to take a few deep breaths immediately before a contest, to free the lungs from residual polluted air and to build up a good reserve of fresh oxygen. How can a horse be persuaded to do the same? The canter down to the start is not enough. The system used with trotters, a proper limbering-up time, is much more sensible.

'Then, of course, a horse at rest breathes abdominally but in the exertion of a race it breathes with the thorax as well ... rather difficult when the saddle is attached with tight girths—and, if the horse has the sense to fill his lungs while being saddled, we return to the attack a few minutes later and tighten the girths even further. Yet the thorax *needs* to be able to expand if the horse is to be able to breathe deeply during a race.

'It is well known that a horse carrying an extra pound in weight over a distance of ten furlongs loses half a length in distance. *We* would never notice if a suitcase weighed a pound more or a pound less—yet a horse weighing five times more than a man, and perhaps ten times as strong, *does* notice. We make him run with nine stone on his back. How would an Olympic athlete perform with a two-year-old child on his shoulders? Some horses weight half as much again as others yet all are expected to shoulder similar weights. Why isn't the weight of the jockey directly related to the weight of the horse?

'The bit! A deliberately cruel implement. Without the bit man would be unable to dominate and subdue a horse.

'When a horse first accepts the bit, little does he know what is in store for him: slavery for life! It is not so cruel if a rider has good hands—but what about those ape-like jockeys who cling to the horse's mouth because they could not otherwise stay in the saddle at all? It must cause torment and suffering for most of the race and then, near the finish, a senseless sequence of tugging and slackening the reins. A dentist puts steel instruments into our mouths which can badly hurt the gums. Sometimes he savagely presses our tongues with that fiendish little mirror—but it only happens to us two or three times a year. Imagine if it were to happen every day!

'Quite apart from the weight of a man, a horse has to contend with his continually changing position, often against his own natural rhythm, especially in amateur races. Even worse are the unexpected sideway movements made by certain jockeys as they use their whips.

'So we come to the whip. Another torture! To hit a horse once, unexpectedly, can be useful because it provokes a flow of adrenalin giving extra energy to the muscles. But of what possible use is the volley of blows inflicted on horses in a hard finish? Usually it just sickens the horse and thereafter he will always connect the whippings with the winning post.' (Tesio was always angered by the thrashings to which many horses were, and still are, subjected.)

A great deal of what Tesio said was true. Although he recognised the impossibility of finding remedies for most of these situations, he would constantly try to invent them and sometimes his inventions worked.

On one occasion Tesio sold a stallion to the Pisa Depot. The horse refused to cover: wheedling, cajolery and urging were to no avail. The Director of the Depot, somewhat discouraged, called on Tesio for assistance. He responded immediately asking to see the mare which the stallion had refused to cover.

'Bring me earth, mud, dust!' he ordered. 'Now make her dirty, muddy, dusty. Rub her all over with straw. Good! Ruffle her mane and tail and leave pieces of straw in them. Perfect! Now take her to the stallion.' As soon as the stallion entered the covering yard, he took one quick look at the mare, threw himself upon her, and covered in a trice!

'You must understand,' Tesio explained afterwards, 'that whilst horses are in training they are educated not to look at the fillies. If they try to approach them they are rebuked and, if necessary, punished. An association of ideas builds up and a brushed and bridled mare, with a well combed mane and tail, becomes "taboo". This poor horse of mine has remembered his lesson only too well!'

Tesio would comment sarcastically on the conventional covering routine and took particular exception to the hobbling of mares and to the fact that, prior to the covering, they were washed down with a sponge soaked in disinfectant. "Suppose *you* were forced to enter a room naked, attached by ropes to two men, one on each side of you. Within, the most beautiful woman in the world awaits you but she is also naked, her ankles held by two ropes which pass through two rings attached to a large collar held tightly by two more men. A third man washes certain parts with a sponge soaked in disinfectant. Do you think you would feel like "doing your duty?" If you did, your two men would force you, by pulling the ropes, to go out the way you came in while the other two men would tow your lady away through a door at the far end of the room. That would be the end of it! This ceremony, always exactly the same, would go on twice a day for five months of the year, with forty different women—young, old, beautiful, ugly. During the rest of the year there would be complete abstinence. What would you produce? Prodigies? Mental defectives to be sure! To this we condemn our mares and our stallions—and we expect them to produce winners!' If his listener demurred saying that this was the destiny of horses, not to be compared with human beings, he had a ready answer envisaging an idyllic scene with forty mares browsing in a large field.

'The stallion with flowing mane and tail, surveying his mares, wanders up, first to one and then to another. One mare ambles away, but he does not follow, another lays her ears and threatens him, a third stays still, turning her head to look at him. The stallion approaches and his attentions are well received. He covers her. Everything is carried out naturally and peacefully.'

This romantic vision fascinated and attracted me so that I asked Tesio why we could not adopt loose covering for our thoroughbreds.

'We have raised them to be stupid so that they would undoubtedly get kicked. And then the stallion owners would never accept the risk. I would not risk it with my mares either—not for fear that they would be hurt but in case the stallion would not accept them. Even amongst our good race mares there are some ugly ones. Have you ever seen girl athletes preparing to race? There isn't much to choose from!'

After this cold shower he gave me another even colder one which caused the idyllic image of the field to evaporate completely.

'The worst part of the conventional routine is that wretched sponge. Have no illusions, love is a question of odour. We are not conscious of the odour but it is there nevertheless. It must be similar to that which dogs smell when a bitch is on heat, although they may be several miles away from her. There are ultra-sonic waves so, probably, there are ultra-olfactory waves too. If not, how do you explain that, of two equally beautiful women, one is successful and the other is not?'

I have said that Tesio's conversation was always amusing and agreeable but the idea that when I had fallen in love it had been due to an olfactory impression, (even if 'ultra-olfactory'), which had produced in me reactions identical to those of a cocker or a labrador, depressed me greatly. Perhaps it would be better to say that Tesio's conversation was always amusing and *almost always* agreeable!

CHAPTER 12

The work

DONNA LYDIA BELIEVED that she was in a position to reveal the "secrets of *rearing* horses' but that it was necessary for me to go to the source, (Tesio), to understand the 'secrets of *training* them'. ('Go to Trenno with him and you'll learn everything.')

Tesio's routine always started early in the day and, shortly after I became co-owner, I commenced, (with confident expectations), sharing his hard-working mornings. When in Milan, Tesio stayed at the old Hotel Europa in the Corso Vittorio Emmanuele. His chauffeur, Battista, would collect him each morning at six o'clock precisely. Tesio was always ready and waiting in the hall a few minutes beforehand. As he was regularly woken at a quarter to six, he evidently jumped out of bed and got straight into the clothes and shoes he had worn the previous day. (No question of a bath.) He did not give the impression of being dirty but never looked well scrubbed or neat. His appearance would be unkempt and crumpled but the impression would be visual, not olfactory! As soon as the car arrived he would get in and if, as was often the case, he had to wait for me, he would make no protest though his face would show impatience.

We would always set off at high speed—only to stop a few hundred yards away at a bar which stayed open very late (or opened very early), and which was patronised by sleepy journalists, noisy taxi drivers, street-sweepers, and newsvendors. Tesio would drink a 'cappuccino' and eat two pastries. (Amazing his fondness for cakes at that early hour.) Unless an observer knew that the route we took to the stables had been that used on the day of Tesio's last victory, it would have seemed ridiculous. (Naturally, after a defeat Battista, the faithful chauffeur, did not need to be told that a particular route, used on the fatal day, must not be used again.)

When we reached the stables the horses would still be in their boxes being given the final touches with a body-brush.

'Enough! Don't torment them! Leave them alone!' was Tesio's invariable exhortation. He understood the sensitivity of a horse's skin and, since his soldier days, thought it fatuous that this process should take so long, (not so much for the sake of the horses but, rather, in order to keep the men occupied).

Tesio was always anxious to have his horses on the training grounds as soon as they opened; he liked to get the best of the going. The horses would emerge from their boxes, the lads already on their backs, to walk around the sand track which encircled a group of buildings in the yard. After one or two circuits, Tesio would order '*Trottooo*', and the horses would break into a trot, some unwillingly, some restlessly, occasionally bucking and plunging. The lads, their faces dark with boredom and sleep, would tug rhythmically at the horses to prevent them overlapping—all too easy in the small crowded circle.

This melancholy merry-go-round would continue for fifteen or twenty minutes—to me it seemed an eternity—but Tesio would sit on a shooting stick, immobile and silent, studying each horse intently. He ignored the lads and their awkward tugging at the horses' mouths, their leathers far too short. He thought them terrible horsemen and tolerated them only as necessary evils. It was torture to me to watch them going round and round, walking, trotting, walking again and, at first, I was unable to understand the purpose behind this rite. When I visited England, some years later, I finally understood. Thoroughbreds all over the world still follow a routine first put into effect by English trainers some 250 years ago—according to which the horses need to be out for at least an hour and three-quarters. In the great English training centres the stables are some distance from the gallops, which are in open country on heath or downland and, after working, the horses are often allowed to graze for a while and to breathe the fresh country air before returning to the monotonous segregation of their boxes.

But, in Milan, the training grounds are only 300 yards from the stables. Trenno and Maura swarm with horses. In order to keep our horses out for the traditional hour and three-quarters, we have a depressing sequence of walking and trotting around the stables in an atmosphere reeking of manure and petrol fumes.

At last it would be time to go to the training grounds and the horses would move off in single file, the head lad in the lead, riding a bicycle. (An Italian head lad would feel humiliated if asked to ride a horse!)

Followed by Tesio's car, the string would move forward in a series of jerks, swerves, bucks and fly-jumps towards the hated place of work. At the Trenno and Maura training grounds every trainer uses a specific sand ring over which he exercises tacit but inalienable rights. When he has finished with it someone else can use it—but woe betide anyone who tries to get there first! When this area was reached the riders would change over, only the best and lightest of them riding the serious work. Rugs and quarter sheets would be removed and work would commence.

Naturally Tesio knew (since it would all have been decided by him) the weight carried by each horse, whether saddles were heavy or light, which men acted as 'brakes', which as 'accelerators', the horse's gait, distance, and prospects of a race. Equally naturally, it would never have crossed Tesio's mind to explain any of this to me. He would be so busy giving instructions and advice and inspecting each animal before, during, and after work, that there would be no time for explanations. The morning work was of vital importance to Tesio; he also enjoyed it. I remember him saying to Donna Lydia and to us, the Incisas: 'Your pleasure is experienced at the afternoon races—mine on the gallops in the morning'. He understood everything involved in the work. I understood nothing.

As soon as the horses left the immediate vicinity of the sand ring, I would lose sight of them and, in the ensuing 'Charge of the Light Brigade', I was, for some considerable time, unable to recognise our own horses—even if they passed in front of us. (When I first started the head lad would sometimes say kindly to me: 'those are ours', but by the time I had picked them out from amongst the hundreds of others, they would have already passed by.) Tesio never said a word and I had to discover from his expression whether the work had pleased him.

After this the weary horses would return to the sand ring sweating, steaming and blowing, with sudden jerks of impatience and wild expressions in their eyes as if to say 'this time you made me do it—but just you try again! Never! Never again!' The head lad and the men would busy themselves with scrapers, sponges and rugs, whistling through their teeth, whilst Tesio would exchange monosyllables with the riders which, however, I was never able to comprehend. The next batch to work would follow immediately—other horses, other work, other impenetrable mysteries for me.

On our return to the stables we would spend time looking in each box and Tesio would inspect any horse with minor ailments. (More subdued mutterings, this time directed to the head lad.) By the time this inspection was over the second lot of horses would be emerging one by one from their boxes; merry-go-round, walk, trot, walk, away to Trenno or Maura, sand ring, change of riders, gallops ...

After the second lot was over, Tesio would return to the city to be shaved (the barber, too, was changed after every defeat), and I would return to Dormello to be greeted by Donna Lydia: 'So—how was it? How did the work go? Tell me everything!'

To this enthusiastic questioning (particularly in the early days) I had no notion how to reply—how to begin, how to continue and, even less, how to end. Even after I had learnt to recognise the horses and to understand what the work was about, I was never much good at describing it in a way which satisfied Donna Lydia. Perhaps for that reason some printed forms appeared one day. The head lad would fill them in, writing down the names of the horses which had worked, their weights, the type of work done by each, and the finishing margins—as well as a few comments: 'easy', 'plenty in hand', 'slow to quicken', 'tired', 'finished well', 'blew a lot'—and so forth. Thereafter I was not asked to make verbal reports.

Sometimes Tesio would return to Dormello with me. During the drive he would never discuss the morning's work. There were the newspapers to read and comment upon, the pedigree book to mull over. Sometimes the two of us would doze off. Then we would arrive. Donna Lydia would meet us—bursting with curiosity: 'Tell me about the gallops! It must have been very exciting!' But Tesio would be ready with a cold shower: 'Wait for the race before you get excited. There isn't much to say about a horse which is ahead of a stable companion in a gallop. It's other people's horses we have to beat, not our own!'

Donna Lydia would be left speechless and mortified as Tesio set off for the village; and the barber.

CHAPTER 13

Training

AFTER A BRIEF period of oppressive and monotonous apprenticeship when, encouraged by Donna Lydia I believed it possible to learn from Tesio how to train horses, I gave up the illusion—and with it the hope that I might one day become his assistant.

Tesio made it clear that, if I wished to see for myself how the training was carried out—if I wished to inspect the condition of the horses or to see the running of the yard—I had, as his associate, every right to do so and I would be welcome at any time. It was equally clear that he did not need my assistance and that he had neither the time nor the inclination to teach me. I resigned myself to the role of observer and, as the daily canters on the sand were of no particular interest to me, I cut down my observances and confined them to selected gallops—those which took place immediately prior to major races.

Tesio, criticized by many and imitated by none, ran these gallops as real trials after the manner of the great English trainers of the nineteenth century. In extreme cases this meant trying a three-year-old classic contender against the four-year-old winner of the previous year's race, at level weights and over the full distance.

The most severe gallops I saw Tesio give were those in which Ettore Tito covered a mile and a half in 2 minutes 34 seconds—*two days* before dead heating with Archidamia in the Gran Premio d'Italia; and two others when Daumier, giving lumps of weight to Tommaso Guidi and Adam, beat both of them over ten furlongs twelve days, and again six days before winning the Emanuele Filiberto.

The experts judged Tesio's methods too harsh and termed him 'knacker', 'butcher', and so on. Tesio ignored the criticisms and disparaging names (if indeed he ever listened at all), and continued along his own road. He believed that horses should run only when they were completely ready and maintained that it was preferable for a horse to lose a race through over-training rather than through under-training. He held that, in the former case, the horse can run again after a couple of months—and win—in the latter event the horse may injure itself or simply be sickened of racing altogether.

Tesio was adamant regarding all-out training and I remember his emphatic remarks to me: "One day, when you have to have a trainer, you will find your horses breaking down during a race—never on the gallops. Through misguided caution the trainer will not have worked them enough. This is a beastly way to carry on, there's nothing worse than to run a horse which is not fit. You have to be as ignorant as "new shoes" not to know that the muscle is elastic and transmits movement through the tendon which is *not*. When the muscle is intoxicated by fatigue, which is more likely the less the horse is trained, it loses elasticity, becomes hard as wood and the tendon is asked to assume the function of shock-absorber. The tendon attempts to take the strain but, that is not its function so, after two or three gallops, it gives and that is the end of your horse! A damaged horse is a horse lost for ever.

'There is no such thing as an "easy race". Neither the trainer, nor the jockey, nor even the horse, make the race, the *other* horses make it. If you tell the jockey to give the horse an easy race and he loses, the public has every right to protest for it is they who keep us in business not, though they like to think so, the directors and officials of countless organisations and associations. So, don't listen to them, listen to me! I try the horses out first, test them thoroughly—and when they race—there is no need to worry, they are ready! And, if in doing so I put an end to them, I am entitled to do so—they're mine!' After a moment's hesitation he added: 'True, they are also yours—but then you agree with me.' It just so happened that I did!

A typical example of severe but, according to Tesio indispensable training, was the case of Navarro. Navarro showed great ability on the racecourse. He won all his races with ease and was made favourite for the Gran Premio di Milano. However, one of his tendons was giving trouble and had begun to bow. Tesio was particularly concerned as Navarro was inbred to Spearmint whose career had been terminated by a similar injury.

There was not much hope for Navarro apart from the tenuous possibility that he might win the race in Milan. Tesio considered that the horse was not fully fit and that a serious gallop was essential to prepare him for the race. For the only time in the history of our partnership Donna Lydia, my wife, and I, were called by Tesio for a consultation. Navarro was led out of his box and it was plain to us all that one of his tendons was indeed bowed.

'If I do not work him,' Tesio said, 'he cannot win and will break down in the race. If I work him he may break down but, if the tendon holds, he will certainly win. You decide!'

We were unanimous, the horse should gallop. It could hardly have been otherwise; despite the courtesy of Tesio's question, the tone did not admit an alternative. After a fabulous gallop Navarro's leg was no worse and the following Sunday he won the race in a canter. On the evening of the race he had broken down completely.

Tesio always timed serious gallops and was, for some reason I never understood, very secretive about it. He kept a stop-watch in his pocket and would glance furtively at it. He attached great importance to the timing and would often point out that: 'A horse at racing pace covers five lengths a second so that, if in an Italian Derby preparation gallop one of my horses were to cover the mile and a half in 2 minutes 34 seconds, people would say "splendid" but, when you consider that Orsenigo ran it in 2 minutes 27 seconds you realise that he would have beaten my horse by 35 lengths! A splendid gallop indeed! What a prospect to sleep on!'

If Tesio were alive today he would probably be amazed to learn that there is not a trainer in Italy who prepares his horses over the full distance they will be called upon to run and, unless they all keep stop-watches hidden in their pockets, none of them time the gallops as he did. I have the impression that the same situation exists in England and in France. It seems strange that, although Tesio's successes remain undisputed and unequalled, his methods have never been imitated and are indeed ridiculed.

Perhaps at this point it would be pertinent to describe one of Tesio's typical gallops, which was epoch-making at Newmarket causing much amazement. It was in 1948 and Tenerani, despite carrying a penalty of 4 lb, had won the Queen Elizabeth Stakes at Ascot. Tesio had gone alone to Ascot and returned to Italy immediately after the race leaving Tenerani in England where he was to contest the Goodwood cup. The horse was transferred to Newmarket and I joined him there. Tesio had given me no specific instructions except to assure me that he would arrive in plenty of time for the important work in preparation for the Goodwood Cup. On his arrival, a week before the race, he went to see the horse and muttered with dismay: 'You've ruined him, he's got far too fat!'

Tenerani appeared normal to me and emaciated to the English who were not used to seeing Tesio's horses. Tesio must have remembered an incident which had occurred the previous year when Tenerani, who on that occasion really was overweight, had been beaten by Zambra, a moderate filly, at Merano. So now, although Tenerani looked far lighter than on the day of that defeat, Tesio insisted that he was too heavy. Now there would have to be some *real* work.

And the real work, over two miles and five furlongs, consisted of using two sprinters, at weight for age, to make the pace for the first five furlongs—at which point Whiteway, winner of the previous year's Cesarewitch, was jumped in to take over for the remaining two miles. The result? Tenerani finished two lengths in front of Whiteway. Mr. James A. Rothschild, a contemporary of Tesio's and a man of considerable knowledge where horses were concerned, afterwards expressed his disappointment at not having seen the gallop and commented that *at last* someone had had the courage to work his horse as the great trainers of the past had done.

I do not know if it was because of this enthusiastic approval but, a few days later, Tesio almost overdid it. The stabling which had been provided for us at Goodwood was several miles from the racecourse so that a horse box was an essential. Although only two days remained before the race, Tesio decided that Tenerani should have another gallop, alone this time, but over the full distance. But, to Tesio's furious disappointment (and to Camici's and my silent satisfaction) the transport which had been arranged failed to appear so that the gallop did not take place.

Tenerani won the Goodwood Cup, beating the hot favourite, Monsieur Boussac's Arbar, by two lengths. Delighted by the victory I made no mention of the gallop which had not taken place but, I am certain that if I had, Tesio would only have replied: 'Yes, but if he *had* had the gallop, he would have won by four lengths instead of two!'

Tesio was exultant. Boussac was furious and said at the time that his horse had broken down. It was all too easy to see that this was untrue and the following day Boussac gave public expression to his rage. Tesio's reply was quoted in the newspapers: 'No one denies that Napoleon was a great general but, in spite of this, Wellington won at Waterloo!' A great many Englishmen had backed Arbar and were not over-enthusiastic about Tenerani's triumph. But they all delighted in Tesio's reply.

The success at Goodwood fully confirmed the value of the ruthless training inflicted by Tesio but, to give some satisfaction to his detractors and to those who said, '*L' è Matt!*' (he's crazy), I write of another occasion on which his methods did not produce the desired results.

Astolfina and Trevisana were to run in the Arc de Triomphe. The two fillies arrived at Chantilly where Mr. Clout, the Comte de Chambure's trainer, had offered them hospitality for the few days before the race. Trevisana had travelled from Milan with a slight cough but Tesio decreed that she should run all the same. She was only there to make the pace for Astolfina, who was 'number one' in our stable having beaten Tenerani in the Gran Premio di Milano.

It had been arranged that, on the Friday, two days before the race, Astolfina should work ten furlongs at half speed with an older horse put at our disposal by Mr.

Clout. Trevisana was to canter nine furlongs on her own. At the last moment, when Mr. Clout's horse had already arrived to accompany Astolfina to the start of the gallop Tesio, instigated by some demon, sent the pacemaker away and ordered our two jockeys, Camici and Caprioli, to take the two fillies to do strong work together over a mile and a half.

Mr. Clout was amazed, I was aghast, and the jockeys muttered their dismay. The two fillies fought out the gallop neck and neck, completing the distance in a ridiculously fast time.

As soon as they returned to the stables, Astolfina started to bleed severely from the nose, having broken a blood vessel. 'Don't worry, I'll soon cure that!' said Tesio and, having been given the address of the nearest chemist, went to consult him about the possibility of coagulating the blood with an enema of isinglass dissolved in hot water. The chemist tried to explain that the walls of the intestines would let the water pass but not the gelatine and that the remedy could not possibly work. Tesio was adamant and left the chemist triumphantly carrying a kilo of isinglass.

On his return to the stable he organised and supervised the preparation and administration—not of *the* enema but *enemas*. In less than two hours the unfortunate Astolfina had been given *fourteen*. According to Tesio a massive dose was necessary. In the end the filly was unable to stand but Tesio continued until the last of the isinglass was gone.

The next day Astolfina was a wreck and Trevisana a ghost for, by now, she not only had a cough but was running a temperature as well. On the day of the race Comte de Chambure was heard to say that one could see 'right through them'. They finished last and last but one.

Astolfina was engaged to run in the Gran Premio del Jockey Club a week after the Arc. The day after the French race, I suggested to Tesio that we should withdraw her. His reply was instant: 'What, not run in the Jockey Club? I'll tear them to shreds—all those wonderful Italian horses!' And Astolfina tore them to shreds!

It had been my idea to run for the Arc de Triomphe and, although Tesio never again referred to the incident at Chantilly, it was the last time that he seriously considered any suggestion of mine. The case of Antonio Canale confirmed this state of affairs.

Antonio Canale had proved a very good horse and his action, which as Donna Lydia said, 'took your breath away', led many (myself included) to suppose that he could be an international champion in the making. Tesio did not agree and, when I repeatedly urged that the horse be sent to Paris for the Grand Prix, he pretended to concede but insisted that a severe gallop over the full distance would be a necessary preparation. In that gallop two of our other good horses were used as pacemakers, one for the first ten furlongs and the other to take it up for the final seven and a half. Antonio Canale flew for the first fourteen furlongs, at fourteen and a half he broke down on one leg, which slowed him down—and at fifteen he broke down on the other leg and came to a complete halt.

Tesio was quite calm (too calm!), and said seraphically, 'Better here than in the race'.

(Riccardo Arpisella, owner and editor of the Italian racing paper *Lo Sportsman*, and a great admirer of Tesio's, had watched the gallop. Afterwards he was heard to exclaim in disbelief: 'He did that on purpose!')

CHAPTER 14

Relationships

I KNEW MOST of Tesio's jockeys: his strong personality never permitted them to become *prima donnas*, as can happen if an owner or trainer is over indulgent.

Federico Regoli had already left the stable by the time I arrived on the scene and his departure was dramatic for Donna Lydia. She had known him since he was born and was his godmother. It was she who had asked that he be christened Federico. For many years he had ridden as first jockey for Tesio and, when increasing weight problems caused him to retire from the saddle, he had remained as Tesio's closest and most trusted collaborator. He was far more than an employee and it was intended that he should ultimately succeed Tesio as trainer. Naturally it was a question of waiting—Tesio was not a man to lay down his arms before falling exhausted on what he regarded as a battlefield. But Regoli did not have the patience. Dormello, then at a comparatively early stage in its history, appeared to be going into a decline and a new stable, which seemed to be coming to the fore, was tempting him to change allegiance. When he and his friend, Caprioli, the stable jockey, went to tell Tesio that the Razza del Soldo had offered them twice as much as they were getting at Dormello, Tesio replied: 'There's the door. Go if you want—but go at once!'

Donna Lydia described this incident to me with tears in her eyes. Tesio merely shrugged.

Caprioli was succeeded by Polifemo Orsini. He was tall for a jockey but was all nerve and muscle. He was arrogant towards his colleagues—an attitude which pleased Tesio as he considered that meekness and tolerance were signs of stupidity if not of dishonesty. 'Let them be generous with their own things, not with mine,' he would say. Orsini had been a jump jockey and was a better horseman than most modern flat jockeys. Tesio greatly appreciated his classic style and Orsini lived up to expectations by winning the Premio Parioli, the Regina Elena, the Oaks, and the Derby with Jacopa del Sellaio— four classics on the same filly, a feat which any present day jockey-acrobat would find hard to match.

Orsini was followed by Romero who had ridden Amur to win the Derby for Radice Fossati. If we agree that the style of riding brought to Europe by the American Tod Sloan really is the best, then Romero was one of its most perfect and instinctive interpreters. He was always perfectly balanced and horses truly flew for him.

Then came Gubellini who had served his apprenticeship under a Mr. Chantre, an old friend of the Tesios. There was no better master than Chantre and all his pupils were known for their impeccable honesty and loyalty.

When Gubellini became Lorenzini's jockey, all of us from Donna Lydia downwards (we Incisas were multiplying) recognised his ability. We did not like him because he beat us too often but, try as we might, we could find no fault with him: he rode well and that was all there was to it. Once Tesio had an objective in view he would never let go. He watched Gubellini and waited, recognising him as a jockey entirely suited to his needs and to his own character.

When eventually Tesio was able to acquire Gubellini, there followed sensational success. Tesio did not criticise Gubellini's riding of Donatello in the Grand Prix—he had ridden to orders—nor did he reproach the jockey for not riding Nearco to orders ... because he won! Had Gubellini not died, after a fall from a horse, Tesio would never have changed jockeys again.

Tesio's last, and perhaps his best jockey, was Enrico Camici. As Tesio's eyesight failed, it was vital to him to have a jockey on whom he could depend entirely. The experienced and excellent Camici carried out his often bizarre and unpredictable instructions to the letter and, during Tesio's last days, Camici's loyalty and exemplary behaviour were an incomparable support.

Another faithful collaborator for the last thirteen years of Tesio's life was Ugo Penco, the head lad. Like Gubellini, Penco had started his career with Chantre and had retained those qualities of application, steadiness and patience which balanced Tesio's impetuous brilliance. Penco kept perfect discipline among the staff which Tesio, absorbed by the horses, ignored completely, and maintained complete authority without ever raising his voice. Penco studied the character of each horse and had a great 'feel' for assessing their limits and possibilities. It was only after Tesio's death, when Penco was promoted to take over the training of the horses, that this great natural gift was fully revealed. But up until that time he would never have presumed to deliver a judgement on a horse or on the management of a race.

Penco's premature and tragic death in a motor accident was an irreparable loss for Dormello-Olgiata. It deprived us of the direct contact we had with the original Tesio tradition and of Penco's own remarkable insight into the character and mentality of the horses. I remember seeing Ribot, a notoriously difficult and capricious horse, walk calmly up a ramp into an aeroplane after his normally placid companion, Magistris, had stubbornly refused to lead the way. I was amazed but Penco commented: 'Typical! Ribot knows when to show that he really is a *man!*'

Tesio's chauffeur led an exhausting life. During the racing season there were constant drives from Milan to Rome, sometimes to Florence and, later in the season, to Naples. Despite the enormous distances and the poor quality of the Italian roads of those days, these trips had to be made in a single stretch.

Battista Zibra was the last of Tesio's chauffeurs. He was an appalling driver who took great pride in the hair-raising speeds he achieved, but whose loyalty and devotion to his master were truly moving. He became the old man's eyes, following the races with the large binoculars which Tesio could no longer use, describing the running as best he could. He became Tesio's factotum and, at the end, his caring and solicitous, if somewhat primitive, nurse.

During Tesio's last months Battista was unsparing in his devotion. In the most tragic and squalid moments of our lives the most wonderful human qualities of people (often those people we have taken most for granted), are revealed. When all appears lost, their consolation and comfort remains. Battista was at Tesio's side night and day and Tesio put himself almost passively into his care.

Among Tesio's associates two other categories must be mentioned. Though not dependants, their services were indispensable to him: I refer to the veterinary surgeons and farriers. Tesio had great respect for the veterinary profession. He would indulge in long discussions with his vets, at which I was often present, and it was clear that the respect was mutual. At the start of these debates Tesio would agree completely with the vet's suggestions but would then lead the conversation through a maze of complicated arguments at the end of which the vet had to pretend being converted to Tesio's own ideas.

The farriers, though they would never openly admit it, tacitly accepted that they were in part his creatures. Before Tesio's time they had shod thoroughbreds in the same way as Italian cavalry horses. It was Tesio who had imported a good English blacksmith to teach the English method to an intelligent young apprentice in Pisa. He learned his trade perfectly and Tesio employed him from then on. He, in turn, taught various apprentices, including his own sons, and we have now reached the third generation of anglicised farriers. Yet Tesio was always present when his horses were shod and was even permitted to make suggestions and give advice—something which would never have been tolerated from any other trainer (farriers are a proud and suspicious breed), but they acknowledged that it was Tesio who had brought their skills to Italy and that he knew what he was talking about.

One day, the day before a big race, Tesio attended the shoeing of his runner. The going was very firm and he decided that it would be wise to put felt between the shoes and the horse's feet. The farrier had no felt with him. Tesio was wearing a hat (from Lock's, no less). 'Give me a pair of scissors!' and he cut several felt half moons from the brim. The hat became a kind of tarboosh—but the next day the horse won his race!

CHAPTER 15

Donna Lydia

IN CHARACTER TESIO and Donna Lydia were almost complete opposites. Whereas Tesio took a perverse delight in intentional blunders and 'putting his foot in it', Donna Lydia was the quintessence of a woman of the world, a defender of conventions.

Public relations were Donna Lydia's specific task— partly because she felt that it was to the benefit of Dormello and the stable but, also, because it satisfied her taste for social life.

Donna Lydia was never beautiful and somehow her dentist had managed to accentuate her resemblance to an old horse. But she had great *style*. She was tall and thin with very pronounced features and enormous feet. She wore country clothes: well cut tweed suits, shoes made to measure, and felt hats—always carefully placed, not just shoved on her head. She also had the ways of a true English lady, owing to the education given her by her mother, an ardent anglophile. Long visits to Victorian England had impressed on her, not only an Anglo-Saxon appearance but also, the manners and language for the role which she felt it was her duty to play.

Each Sunday, after Mass in the little church at Dormello, as the congregation was making its way out, Donna Lydia would remain for a few moments, absorbed in prayer—her face buried in her hands. When the priest had removed his vestments, she would go to pay her 'filial' respects, rather in the spirit in which Franz Joseph, resplendent in a field-marshal's uniform, covered with decorations, would follow the blessed sacrament in procession through the streets of Vienna.

Nobody knew where this aristocratic bearing came from. Her father was a gentle Dalmatian shipowner (today he would be Jugoslav, at that time his ships sailed under the Austrian flag), who, rather late in life, had married a very beautiful Neapolitan girl considerably younger than himself. His marriage brought him the title of Marchese di Serramezzana. (Although this title cannot today be found in any register of the nobility, it must have existed for it to have been passed on to her son, Stefano,— and then died out with him. Certainly Elena, who won the Italian Derby, was listed as having belonged to the Marchese di Serramezzana.) They settled in Florence, where Donna Lydia's father had to adapt himself to the way of life which pleased his young wife. They kept open house and gave balls and receptions. When the 'gentle Dalmatian shipowner' had had enough, he would encourage his guests to leave with phrases which have remained famous in Florence: 'Well, it's over you've eaten, you've drunk, it's time to go home!' Or 'Eleven o'clock— and there's no sign of rain!'

Donna Lydia's wealthy parents had brought her up to a luxurious way of life but, at Dormello, Tesio's rigid regime meant that every last penny was made available to the stud. To have only one man-servant was a great concession on the part of Donna Lydia but, as that man-servant was the chauffeur, and she believed that a butler was essential to the dignity of a household, she had to go one further and be satisfied with dressing *him* in a white jacket with red epaulettes, (the stable colours), to serve at table. (Afterwards he would rapidly change into a blue uniform for the drive into Milan for the races.)

On very special occasions a simpleton named Primo was engaged to act as footman. (This was more for show than use since he was incapable of understanding or doing much.) He too was dressed in a white jacket. (On one occasion Donna Lydia had entertained four or five guests, all, as she was, in their late seventies. During the night thieves broke into the house, stole the silver objects from the table in the drawing room and, after emptying two cushions of all their feathers, used the covers to carry off their booty. The next morning Primo found feathers all over the place. He accepted the situation at its face value, exclaiming: 'Goodness, how the masters must have enjoyed themselves last night!')

Donna Lydia was a most agreeable hostess—but with an exact sense of caste according to which she decided who was or was not acceptable at her table.

Very early in our association she gave me precise instructions on the attitude I should adopt towards our employees. After a splendid victory Gubellini (our jockey) held out his hand—and I clasped it warmly. Donna Lydia took me aside and admonished me maternally, but quite firmly: 'You must not shake hands with the jockeys! Whatever are we coming to? If he holds out his right hand, put your right hand on his left shoulder and say a few kind words such as "Well done, my lad. You rode well!" That way you will teach him a lesson and put him in his place without hurting his feelings.' (To back up her admonition regarding the correct attitude I should adopt towards such employees, Donna Lydia would tell me a story related to Fred Archer, the champion jockey. Some owners had been walking towards the gates of their Kingsclere stables. The trainer, John Porter, called to

Fred Archer who was standing near by: 'What are you
doing standing there? Why don't you run and open the
gates for these gentlemen?' Archer blushed for shame,
opened the gate, stood aside, and waited until the last
visitor had passed through.)

Donna Lydia's attitude towards the staff was maternal
in a dignified way. She maintained an air of detachment
except on family occasions such as christenings, first
communions and weddings. Marriage was gone into very
thoroughly at Dormello and the girl's past had to be
investigated before an engagement could be announced.
Provided this test was passed, there was a ceremony of
presentation to Donna Lydia when the engaged couple
were received in the drawing room of the villa. (Everyone,
however, remained standing.) I think Donna Lydia felt
that, the longer the engagement, the higher the moral
standards of the pair and the fact that there was no
urgency was considered a guarantee.

Her behaviour was not due to pride or arrogance: it
was dictated by a profound and sincere conviction that she
had a function to carry out—her duty in 'that state of life
into which it had pleased God to call her'.

One asks oneself why, given her point of view, Donna
Lydia had ever considered marrying Tesio who was, at the
time, only a gifted young dare-devil. I only know that it
all started with the friendship between Tesio and Stefano
Flori and their mutual interest in gambling, horses and
racing. Donna Lydia had horses which ran under her own
colours. Doubtless it was their shared interest in horses
which had brought two very different beings together for
life.

Donna Lydia always kept the register of the mares
up-to-date. It was a huge volume bound in red hide across
which was printed in gold lettering, 'Printed by the

Kruszynski Stud, property of the Princes Lubomirski'. Inside, each sheet carried headings: Name, Colour, Date of Birth, Pedigree of Mare. And, lower down, on successive subdivisions, the pedigrees of each stallion which had covered the mare, year by year, and observations on the offspring. The notes were concise and laconic, rarely flatering and often ruthless. I recollect on one page comments on the offspring of a mare which read:

> First foal: Useless roarer
> Second foal: Useless non-roarer

I can imagine Donna Lydia's pitiful protests as she transcribed these cruel verdicts—and Tesio's obstinate refusals to alter them.

In September, 1974, thieves again broke into Dormello; the villa was empty by then. They somehow managed to remove the large and very heavy old table on which the big book always lay. When I was informed by telephone of the theft, I was told that two pictures had gone as well as the table and—'only (only!) a few books'. I resigned myself to the fact that the remarkable relic was lost and, during my frequent visits to Dormello, I did not even go into the room. When I finally entered it in 1975, I was overjoyed to see that the register was still there. Apparently it had been found on the floor. It was just as it had been left when Donna Lydia stopped compiling it. Having been dipped into and consulted incessantly over a lifetime, its condition was far from perfect. The binding was peeling and partly detached, some of the pages were curled up, others torn, and the lower corners had become darkened by frequent turning.

I was delighted to have found it and looked through the pages to make sure they were all there. I was moved at seeing those entries again—written in Donna Lydia's large handwriting but in a style which was typical of Tesio—kept carefully up-to-date, starting with Velika, Saphirine, Tenebreuse, right down to Buonamica, Romanella, Trevisana, well-known names—but so many others which remained obscure but which caused just as much work. All the work, the care and the attention—only to discover at the end of it that you probably have a useless brute on your hands. For some owners, either more resigned or less involved, such set-backs would have been no more than disappointments. Others would have found excuses for the horses or admitted their own errors in choosing the wrong matings or giving the wrong training.

Not so Tesio! He had neither doubts nor regrets. He knew that *he* had done all for the best: 'I have done so much for you and you are useless. Damned horse!'

And Donna Lydia, who did not share these views or understand this intemperance of speech, meekly transcribed imprecations and maledictions because it was *he* who uttered them—and *he knew*.

This complete lack of personal opinions led me to believe that Donna Lydia made a conscious renunciation, that she wished to be passive as a homage to Tesio, to devote herself completely to him. It seems impossible, considering the life she led at Dormello and her love for the horses, that she should not have had opinions of her own. I believe that, if she had been alone, though she could never have equalled Tesio's achievements, she would have risen to the level of the best bloodstock breeders in Europe.

Instead, when she was alone at Dormello, often for long periods, she would start the day be getting all the news from the stud-groom, then she would settle down to her voluminous correspondence, deal with Tesio's instructions (of which she kept a complete record), and afterwards she would play solitaire interminably. From the cards she would try to discover the answers to many questions: 'Shall we win the race tomorrow?' 'Shall we win the Derby this year?' 'Next year?' She did not really believe in this. She was devoutly religious and not at all superstitious but this game reflected an almost obsessive concern for everything which made up the very reason for her existence—Dormello, the racing stable, the prestige and honour of Tesio's name. This was a 'whole' which was embodied in *him*.

Her abdication, her desire to be *nobody* in front of him, was the aspect of Donna Lydia's character which was most appealing and most unforgettable.—And it is through her, through her great red book, through her handwriting—at first clear and strong, and at the end, after having written so much for him, uncertain and almost illegible—that a faithful image of Tesio is handed down to us.

CHAPTER 16

Epilogue

WHEN PEOPLE ASK me questions about Tesio they usually want confirmation of myths concerning him and information about his horses (always the most famous ones). They do not realise that, in order to produce this select handful, Tesio had to raise 700 or 800 and that, for every one of that 700 or 800, he studied, planned and worked just as hard as for the stars. Such people do not understand that, apart from the 50-odd hours of each year when the public saw him at the racecourses, he spent 2,500 hours in the stable, on the training grounds, or alone with his thoughts, hopes, preoccupations and disappointments.

Tesio's life, despite all the dramas and successes, was essentially and drearily monotonous. Every day for 50 years he woke up at dawn. Then came first outing ... stable; second outing ... stable; lunch, alone at a modest inn; siesta; again the stable; sometimes, only sometimes, a cinema; dinner ... or, to punish himself after a defeat, he would fast and retire early to bed.

Four wars, the German occupation, the fall of Fascism and the Italian monarchy, the setting up and disappearance of great new stables (some more magnificent than his) may have worried or irritated him, but they never disturbed his unchangeable routine.

The enterprise had been created by him alone. Donna

Lydia's little stable and his grandmother's villa had been liquidated to found Dormello. He was not only its master and absolute autocrat, but also its only brain. The rest of us, including Donna Lydia, were not equals: we were 'subordinates' of various categories, classes, and conditions, and we did not always understand at what he was aiming. Tesio did not run his undertaking like a Pirelli or an Olivetti. He was a Michelangelo, a Leonardo. True, they also had assistants, but only to sketch rough drafts and grind colours.

Today, in an era of gigantic industrial concerns, businesses run by a single man and directed by a single brain are derisively described as 'artisan'. Tesio started Dormello as an artisan concern. He was its sole creator and it remained an artisan concern even after the Dormello-Olgiata Company Limited was set up, and for as long as Donna Lydia registered profits and losses in her naïve notebook which made the experts smile.

I often saw Tesio do manual work in the stables when an urgent operation was required for an injured horse, or when he wished to show a lad the best procedure. Few knew of this, often manual, work. He would frequently say to me: 'you can't manage a racing stable properly if you are not ready to spend the whole day amid the stench of litter'. He said 'stench' not 'smell', because another peculiarity of his was that, although he lived perpetually amongst horses, he would carefully wash his hands if he touched a single animal.

Once, I cannot remember after which defeat, Tesio spoke to me about his monotonous, exhausting daily work, of which most people were unaware.

'In an empty theatre, on a bare stage, the actors work on their own, repeating the same dialogue for days and weeks. How many people go to the rehearsal of show?

Very few! Then, on the first night, the public in their comfortable seats claim the right to judge both the author and the actors "because they have paid for their tickets". But what is the price of a ticket compared with the apprehension and anxiety of the actors? And so we are alone on the training grounds watching our horses, day after day, week after week, whatever the weather, in all seasons, repeating canters and gallops over and over again, working ... toiling. Who comes to see the work in the mornings? Nobody, apart from the occasional trainer. Then, on the day of the race, the public on the stands feel they have the right to express judgments about the trainer or the losing favourite. Sportsmen? Far from it! They are a Colosseum public who gloat when a favourite is beaten and who come to the jumping meetings hoping to see a nasty fall!'

But apart from such rare outbursts there were no recriminations, no complaints about the past. He would say: 'I have made a mistake; I should have been more careful! I shouldn't have believed them! I shouldn't have listened to him!' He was accusing himself and each misfortune stimulated him to discover the remedy: '*Now* I know what I'll do next time!'

Tesio was never conceited or pretentious. He went his own road, never saying 'this is the right way'. This is, perhaps, why so few understood him and no-one followed him. In these pages, even if I have only been able to show incidents, actions, and reactions, I did not mean to emphasise what Tesio *did*. Everyone knows that. I wanted to convey what Tesio *was*, what he had within him, how exceptional a man he was.

Too much has been said in the past about his successes, his achievements and his good luck; too little about his will, his determination and his perseverance. And too little about his humanity—some people made a hero out of Tesio and heroes must not be human. What a man is matters much more than what he does.

As during his life Donna Lydia had backed, supported, and defended Tesio, so, after his death, she jealously guarded his memory in order that the inheritance he left should not be wasted and that Dormello-Olgiata should remain. But Tesio could not imagine that these creatures of his would continue after his death.

He made this clear on two occasions: first when the deed for setting up Dormello-Olgiata was drafted. The lawyer, trying to get him to accept an innovation, said that one day 'from Heaven' he would have the consolation of seeing the continuation of his 60 years' activity on earth. Said Tesio: 'From Heaven? Of what interest do you think horses will be to me from Heaven?'

The second time was in 1953 when he was in great pain and had been transferred to the clinic a few days before his death. Donna Lydia told him that Ugo Penco, the head lad, was at the door to give to him the latest news from the stable. Retorted Tesio, feebly: 'To Hell with horses and stable!'

*   *   *   *

It must have been in 1952 or 1953 ... Tesio's last years, when he no longer spent the winters at Pisa. Dormello, so pleasant and delightful in spring and summer, becomes dismal and gloomy in autumn and winter; the trees are dark and funereal in the rain and mist, and the grass loses its colour.

This was Dormello when I arrived one evening. All the shutters were closed and the glass doors were barred and bolted as though the house was uninhabited. But I knew this was not so. I knocked and, after a long while, the door was opened by Donna Lydia's chauffeur-butler. The entrance hall was as cold as the outdoors, the pantry, through which we had to pass, was lukewarm because it was next to the kitchen. From there I went into the hothouse atmosphere of the dining-room.

No changes had been made except that a large stove had been installed, the cause of the sweltering heat. The only source of light was a standard lamp with a large lampshade at one end of the room. Two motionless figures were seated on either side of this—the Tesios.

He was sunk in an armchair, exactly as I had seen him for the first time at the Hotel Plaza in Rome 30 years before. He was immersed in a book just as he had been then. His legs were wrapt in a plaid rug, he was wearing a heavy coat, he had a woollen scarf around his neck and on his head ... what was he wearing? Certainly something incongruous, perhaps a very large beret. I had never seen him wear it, even outside the house; indoors it seemed quite absurd.

Donna Lydia wore a large, old, black fur coat. She had a thick rug over her knees and was sitting at a bridge table on which were spread the cards for a game of solitaire— this she played when she was unable to indulge in her favourite pastime, conversation.

There was something lugubrious about the semi-obscurity of the room, the stale air and the two people who seemed encumbered by all those garments. We exchanged news: about people with her, about horses with him. Then Donna Lydia returned to her cards.

Tesio became more and more excited, speaking of mares due to go abroad, of foalings which would soon take place, about coverings, and about the stallions and colts at Olgiata.

'We must ...,' he said.

'We must!' He was 83 or 84 years old and, still thinking about the future, he roused himself from the semi-torpor of a few moments before. No reference to the past, no recollection of what he had done in 60 years of restless activity, no regrets, no sorrow, no thought of death: only plans for the future.

'We must ... we ought to ...'

Always what ought to be done, that duty which he had spontaneously and freely accepted and which still spurred him on to plan, foresee, arrange. His eyes were dim, his voice weak, his reactions slow. But behind these appearances there was still the same Tesio, the man who, all his life, had said to himself: 'I must ... I ought to ...'